WHEN DO I SEE GOD?

WHEN DO I SEE GOD?

Finding the Path to Heaven

JEFF IANNIELLO

RAINBOW RIDGE
BOOKS

Cover and interior design by Frame 25 Productions
Cover photograph © Bruce Rolff c/o Shutterstock.com

Published by:
Rainbow Ridge Books, LLC
140 Rainbow Ridge Road
Faber, Virginia 22938
434-361-1723

If you are unable to order this book from your local bookseller, you may order directly from the distributor.

Square One Publishers, Inc.
115 Herricks Road
Garden City Park, NY 11040
Phone: (516) 535-2010
Fax: (516) 535-2014
Toll-free: 877-900-BOOK

Visit the author at:
www.sitelane.com

Library of Congress Cataloging-in-Publication Data applied for.

ISBN 978-0-9844955-5-9

10 9 8 7 6 5 4 3 2 1

Printed on acid-free recycled paper in the United States of America

To Joan, for bringing part of heaven to earth

CONTENTS

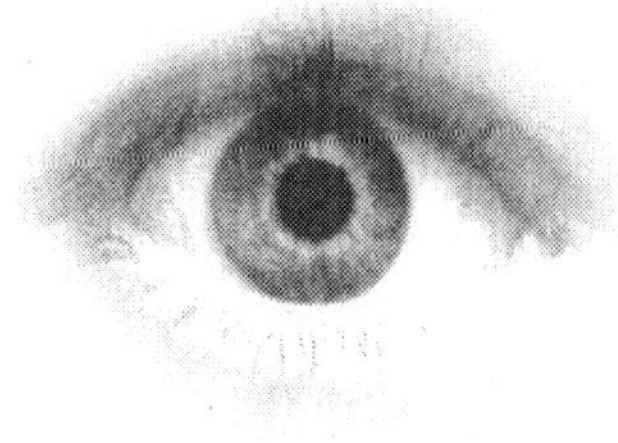

INTRODUCTION

When I set out to write this book, I intended to describe my beliefs regarding the afterlife. Essentially, I hoped to explain what heaven would be like. The change from a physical existence to a spiritual one would obviously require a change in perception. I also hoped to expand my own understanding as to the power of imagination and consciousness freed from a mortal body.

Unfortunately, I did not believe I would be able to hold an audience's interest for long if I simply tried to write a dry narrative. The differences in life experiences and expectations would also prove to be a difficult burden to overcome. How could I share my beliefs of a joyous, fulfilling afterlife with others that certainly have different backgrounds, hopes, and desires?

At one point, I considered trying to express my expectations as if describing a dream. The idea held merit, but only to a point. Utilizing a dream could assist in separating material existence from imagination, but it did not go far enough. I wanted to ensure a clear difference between a dream world and the afterlife.

Instead, I decided to utilize a story about a man who dies suddenly and steps into a spiritual existence. Through this story, I could depict the moment of death and the switching of consciousness from a physical world to a spiritual one. The main character is fictional, but I utilize him as a tool to explain my expectations of the afterlife. The character in the story would experience the aspects of a true heaven, and there would be no confusion as to whether he was caught in a dream state or existing in an afterlife.

As the story unfolded in my mind, I began to examine not only the facets of a spiritual existence in comparison to a physical one, but connections between the two planes. The story quickly shifted from an individual's spiritual journey into an internal conflict as to what actually constituted heaven. Leaving the physical plane means more than simply adjusting perceptions to meet a soulful existence. It also means accepting the limitless scope of consciousness unbounded by any material objects.

Such acceptance may not come immediately. Barriers created during lifetimes in this world may not simply disintegrate upon the first step into the afterlife. Holding to those barriers would prove to be an obstacle for truly experiencing heaven.

A large barrier that became clear to me was my own continuing doubts regarding the nature of this physical world. To me, an acceptance of heaven means an acceptance of God. An understanding of God, however, is blurred by doubts that rise out of conditions existing right here on earth.

Thus, the story evolved. It was no longer about a man's simple journey into heaven, but a probable scenario for those that hold on to doubts about the nature, or even the very existence, of God.

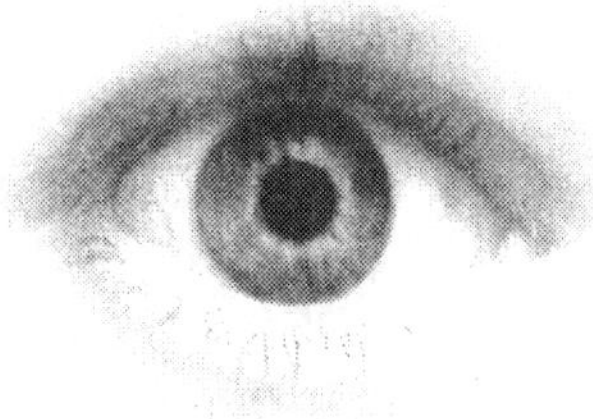

DEATH

By chance or by design, the consequences of an action unseen can have a far reaching impact, even beyond all reasonable intentions. As unlikely as he might have ever imagined, one man's fate rested in the ground beneath a tree far removed from his sight, and his journey into the next life began with a storm.

Heavy rains swept away the dirt supporting the roots of a large tree, and in mere moments, the mature oak collapsed into the surrounding muck with the same majesty as a giant crocodile thrashing about in quicksand. Sharp cracks from the snapping of several branches added cymbal-like crashing emphasis to the constant patter beat of the rain, but the tree's impact with the ground resounded with more of a dull thud than any dramatic sounding concussion.

As fate would have it, the heavy tree fell across the banks of a small stream, covering the waterway fully from side to side. With the rain feeding not only this tributary but many of the creeks and brooks that ultimately emptied into it, the current raced with a maniacal flow and the water deepened into a heavy torrent. The trunk, as well as the thick branches that dangled into the stream, quickly trapped more mud and debris flushed up within the now blocked waterway. A dam formed, not without leaks, but enough of an obstruction to divert more than half of the flowing current over the stream's banks and back into the nearby stagnant lake that was the main source of the stream's waters.

This larger body of water was actually a manmade reservoir and the stream served as an outlet to handle seasonal overflows. With the stream significantly blocked, there was no clear passage for the rising waters.

The surface level of this reservoir was also being fed by the heavy rainfall and it had already reached a point well above the recognized flood stage. The additional water from the backed up stream increased the pressure on the elevated banks that kept the lake contained. At the southeast corner, the mound began to break apart. The embankment eventually disintegrated and fell away as a thick layer of muddy sludge. Crumbling, bubbling, and oozing in front of the frenzied current, the slushy muck preceded the first breakaway flood waters that barreled down the hillside.

The water broke from a breach that at first appeared inconsequential at best, but the crashing flow quickly widened the gap. As the breach expanded, the amount of water surged in both weight and force. The downward slope of the hillside served to add speed and power to the growing wave, and the flash flood now tumbled down the hillside with a grinding, churning energy that far surpassed the original overflow from the small stream.

The hillside was adorned with only grass, and this simply bent to the ferocity of the surging flow. Nothing blocked the path of the flash flood until it hit a small grove of trees several hundred yards past the base of the first hill. Dozens of saplings broke under the force and became lodged between the trunks of those larger trees around them. These obstructions created breaks in the current, forged small barricades that held against the surging water. As these barriers served to temporarily restrict the growing swell, large pools began to form that were now being fed not only by the flood waters from the broken embankment, but also by the deluge of rain.

The pounding downpour soaked the ground. The soil could absorb no more and now additional surface water rushed down the surrounding hillsides and joined with the deepening pools. The water that collected in the twisting valleys of the hills measured several feet deep and it continued to rise behind the obstructions within the trees.

Beyond this barricade, the muddy sludge that served as the herald for the initial flood wave continued to rush forward. Pressed on by water that continued to flow freely, it tumbled along the bases of the hills. The wide, gurgling mass of thick mire twisted and turned as it searched for lower and lower ground. Its speed was deceptive. From a distance, it appeared to move slowly, almost like thick volcanic lava leisurely bubbling down a mountainside. In truth, it raced forward much more swiftly than appearances would reveal.

Eventually, the thickened head of the flood waters reached the banks of a nearby river. The river itself was already swollen from the heavy rains. The light brown water tumbled about in swift currents just as the falling raindrops adorned the flowing surface with thousands and thousands of small circular blasts of upheaval.

As the waters finally tumbled over the bank, the sludge marking the beginning of the flash flood simply vanished into the churning torrent of the river, broken apart and swept away by the faster and more powerful current. The first entrance of these flood waters into the river made no discernable change in the volume of muddy liquid passing between its banks. This, however, was only temporary.

Back at higher ground—beyond many of the hilltops that separated the lake from the river and above the grove of trees that now marked a new pool of deepening water—the broken edges of the embankment collapsed much further and the gap tripled in size. In one giant wave, a much larger swell of water charged down the hillside. It hit the growing pools trapped behind the fallen trees with a monumental crash. The force ripped apart everything in its way, including those trees that survived the first onslaught. The flood surged onward with renewed power as nothing remained to restrict its flow.

With the only obstruction cleared, the gurgling, foaming waters raced angrily around the hill bases with the fury of a stampede. When this second wave finally hit the river and raced into the channel, it appeared to ride over the top of the currents that ran between the banks.

The flash flood now carried broken tree trunks and heavy limbs, along with the churning mud and untold gallons of water surging forward with immense force. When the natural river bank curved full to the east, the torrent broke containment once more and the charging flood continued on a southeasterly course. The heavy debris rolled over the barren river edge and on to a small flood plain that had already been saturated and filled to capacity.

Behind the now massive wall of water, the heavy currents of the river grew and continued to nourish the once again freed flood. The released wave hit a small country road and barreled down this empty path directly toward a small home with a single occupant.

Steven Drilach didn't much care one way or the other about the rain. He had nothing planned that evening, so what did he care? Weather was beyond his control, so it wasn't worth grumbling about. Yes, storms could be a nuisance at times, especially snow storms. He hated shoveling the white stuff, particularly when it was heavy and slushy, but he never had to shovel rain, so he remained undeterred in his indifference to the whole event. He even managed to keep a positive outlook as he muttered to himself that if it didn't rain, the grass around his small home would dry up and turn brown.

Rather than lamenting about any inconvenience, he took

advantage of the time he now had to himself. He sat alone in his living room reading a rather curious novel with enough plot twists to keep him intrigued and guessing at the author's ultimate message. The heavy downpour outside offered a pleasant percussion concerto in the background with a rhythmic pounding of rain against his roof. He never actually noticed, but his eyes scanned the written words before him in a tempo that matched the beat of the raindrops. In essence, his mind became unconsciously tied to the elements outside, and he remained at peace with the world around him until the storm itself decided to break that serenity.

In the distance, he heard a strange sound like the throaty growl of some long extinct dinosaur. Initially, he thought it was thunder, but the clamor did not diminish and he had not seen any flash of lightning. He listened with greater focus as a frown of discontent shaped his features. He had become attuned to the simple drumming of the rain on the exterior of his house, embraced it as a friend to share the evening. This rumble was not so welcome and it shredded his attention, grated at his nerves. As if to add mystery to his unspoken consternation, the internal lights to his home flashed, once . . . twice . . . and then went out completely.

At first, this seemed to confirm his suspicion about a lightning strike, but the rumbling in the distance never waned. Instead, it grew.

If he had a candle nearby, he might have simply lit it and continued his reading in a comfortable solitude that was now enhanced by the darkness around him. Steven, however, had no such item nearby, nor did he have a match with which to light it. He also could not block out the growing roar that sounded now almost like a freight train at full throttle.

Steven wanted to check his front window, but not enthralled by the prospect of stumbling about in the dark, he moved first toward another objective.

Rising out of his living room chair and placing the book he was reading down upon the abandoned seat cushion, he strode carefully through the darkened archway into the kitchen. He could see the rain pounding against a side window, but the rhythmic smattering of raindrops pelting the glass was now all but drowned out by the expanding roar.

Before he could reach the cabinet where he kept his flashlight, his home began to shake. That was the last thing he remembered of this world. The wave of water hit the front of his house and the lonely little dwelling was swept aside almost instantly by the force.

Twisting, cracking, and crunching, nearly every component of the kitchen swelled in vicious upheaval as if a bulldozer crashed into the far wall at breakneck speed. The floor buckled under Steven's feet just as dust from the crumbling ceiling clouded the air. With cabinets turning to splinters and appliances groaning in twisted metal, debris of every type fell upon him in a surge of mayhem. His body was crushed before his clothes even became damp from the rushing waters.

Death was not painful for Steven and his last emotion was one of confusion, not fear or dread. The realization that he was about to die never entered his mind, for he dropped into unconsciousness almost immediately. If all awareness was to end upon death, he never would have known that he died in a flood. Of course, he would very soon discover that the death of the body does not necessarily lead to the end of existence or consciousness.

The house broke into several pieces, most of which rode the currents of the flash flood into the surrounding streets. The roof stayed almost entirely intact, but it was quickly separated from the rest of the structure. It came to rest in a wooded area a short walk from where it used to sit upon walls that now no longer existed. Scraps of furniture, saturated books and files, chunks of electronic equipment, and pieces of clothing floated much further along with the current and littered storm drains and creak beds for miles.

Steven's body was stuck within the compacted remains of what used to be his kitchen, dining room, and back bedroom.

This large mass of crushed wood, plaster, siding, and insulation also ended up in the woods, but much further down the road than the rooftop.

Back in the hills, the flood waters receded quickly once the level of the reservoir fell below the bottom of the breach. With this area of ground more solid and with less pressure placed upon it from the dwindling water level, the lower embankment held. No further water raced down the hillside other than that of the diminishing rain.

The churning mass of water that previously flowed through the now destroyed grove of trees weakened to a slow stream and then to a mere trickle. Very soon, the remnants of the flood waters failed to make it out of the valleys within the hills and turned to still pools in thick grass or heavy mud surrounding broken tree trunks.

No additional water broke upon the river and the level of the rushing current racing between its banks dropped quickly. Without the flood waters feeding the tide, the river remained within its natural channel and no further surge escaped its banks.

The flood plain at the eastern river bend became still, turning into a deathly quiet pool of trapped water, and the dark gray asphalt of the country road leading to Steven's house channeled the last remnants of the flash flood off to drainage ditches and storm drains.

Local authorities discovered Steven's house, or rather the empty concrete slab of the foundation, rather quickly. Emergency crews followed the destructive path of the flood and spotted the roof and another major portion of the now demolished structure firmly entrenched into a thicket of trees.

Steven's body was not located until the proper equipment could be dispatched to break up the crushed remnants that entombed him. He was pronounced dead at the scene.

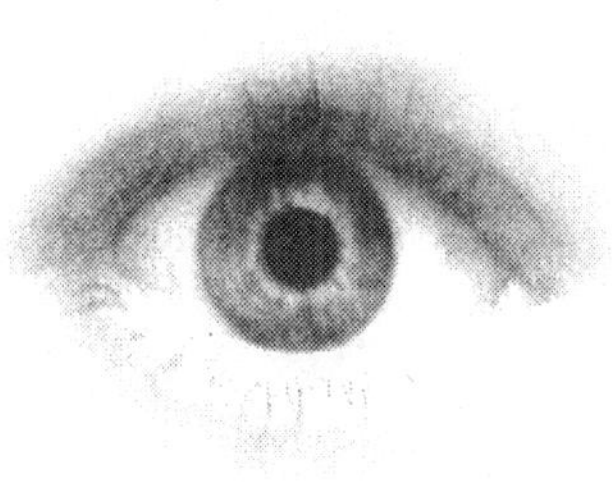

CONSCIOUSNESS

The precise moment of Steven Drilach's death was neither euphoric nor horrifying. There was no egregious tearing in the fabric of reality as if his soul was ripped from his body like flesh from the bone and then thrust unwillingly into a dark and shadowy realm. On the other hand, there was also no chorus of waiting angels delicately lifting his spirit through a tunnel of bright light and into the loving hands of previously past friends and relatives.

For Steven, the transition was a simple step from one plane of consciousness into another, an unobtrusive event that barely created a ripple of significance in either dimension. Other than his mortal body, everything that he was, the very essence of his identity and existence, passed over from one realm into the next, and that transition began at the exact instant his body ceased to sustain life.

Steven's last moments on earth were not painful ones. He went through such trauma that he died instantly from the calamity caused by the flood. The impact from the objects around him broke his bones, crushed his organs, and forced the blood from his veins and tissue. Despite this violent mayhem—or more accurately, because of it—there was no cognitive moment of severe pain and distress. The heart ceased to beat just as the impulses within his brain stopped, as if a light switch had simply been turned to the off position. The spark of life that served as the connection between his spirit and his body, the glue that kept his soul in the physical world, was extinguished in the bat of an eye.

With his time on earth complete, his ultimate end reached and concluded beyond doubt, his link to the material world broke away clean. His spiritual essence moved on to the next phase of consciousness. It was not as if he stepped through a door, flew through some portal, or slipped past the veil of infinity. His awareness simply moved, ended its focus in one world and began its existence in the next.

For Steven's consciousness, the transition was seamless. One moment he was in his kitchen. The next instant, he stood upon the flat, hard floor of what appeared to him as a large empty room.

At the initial moment of transference, he did not hold a true understanding of what had just happened to him. His mind buzzed with a realization that something had occurred, he just didn't know what it was. His thoughts were initially wiped clean, but slowly, reflective considerations gently filled his consciousness.

It was not overwhelming confusion he felt at that moment, though certainly some questions nagged at him, and despite the nature of his circumstances, he did not experience terror or anxiety. As if to hold things in perfect balance, there also wasn't any impression of glorious awe or triumphant delight. In fact, his emotional response seemed almost inappropriate. He didn't feel lost and he didn't feel as if he just returned home from some long journey. Truth be known, he truly lacked any significant reaction to this most perplexing moment—no pain or comfort, no joy or sadness, no great amusement or heavy despair. If pressed for his own definition, he would have stated he felt indifference, if such a thing could truly be felt.

The wide range of his previous earthly emotions compacted themselves into a sparse set of simple sensations that allowed him to reflect clearly on his present condition. He knew who he was; remembered his name and his identity. In fact, he retained all the memories of his previous existence. These memories, however, just could not explain his present situation.

He stood in a place he could not recognize, a place with no apparent purpose, and he stood alone.

Without moving beyond craning his neck in several directions, he surveyed his surroundings. The hard floor extended beneath him in all directions. It remained flat and level until it reached the bases of plain white and unmarked walls. These walls surrounded him in a simple but large rectangular formation. In the distance and in several different locations, he noticed stairwells with steps leading both up and down. He could not see where these led. To his left within one of the walls, he saw one solid paneled door. It was simple in décor, plain and white, just like everything else. It remained closed.

The space about him looked much like the concrete platform for a subway train, except there was no deep channel for the tracks. There were also no other waiting passengers, no turnstiles and no benches, and no guards or ticket booths with occupants waiting to accept tokens. He stood quite alone in this wide expanse.

Continuing his inspection of the walls in the distance and the floor below him, Steven wondered about their composition. The ground appeared like some kind of stone, but the surface was not rough like concrete, nor was it slippery smooth like marble. Perhaps the floor consisted of white slate, for it felt hard and solid beneath his feet. He could not guess as to the walls. He remained too far away to get a close enough look to make any sound judgment. They appeared like ordinary sheetrock, with the seams spackled flawlessly and any imperfections well sanded away.

As he inspected the area, he realized he could find no light fixtures. The walls and ceiling, however, appeared bright just the same, as if they were self-luminous. The walls were solid with no windows and thus no rays of sunshine angled down into any distant corner. Still, light fell about the area from all directions, not from one source, but seemingly from everywhere at once. The brightness held to a uniform degree, keeping the entire room glossed in consistency as if darkness was not allowed. Looking upon the ground, he noticed his form made no distinct shadow.

He slowly stepped about in a small circle, turning and examining the space around him. His steps made small thumps upon the stone floor and this was the only sound he could hear. An empty silence waited for him everywhere else.

"Hello?"

He heard his own voice, but there was no echo.

Nothing . . . no response from any direction welcomed or even challenged his presence.

The questions that nagged at Steven's consciousness took greater hold of his thoughts.

Where am I?

How did I get here?

He could not answer either of these questions.

This realization did not bring a sense of peril. His body did not tense in panic and his mind did not cloud with apprehension. He simply recognized he now stood in a place he could not identify, and he could not fathom as to how he got there. Acknowledging these facts simply demanded further consideration.

Concentrating on the last thing he could remember, an image of his small home came to his mind. He recalled the failure of the lights and his attempt to retrieve a flashlight. He even remembered the distant rumble growing into a deafening crash and the kitchen seemingly coming apart around him. That was all his mind could retrieve.

Wondering what might have happened in those last moments, he looked down upon himself and he realized he was wearing different clothes than he remembered. He had on sneakers, jeans, a T-shirt, and a sweatshirt. This was not what he recalled wearing when he rose from the living room chair and put down his novel in the dark. He recognized all the garments he currently wore. The clothes were indeed his, and they were comfortable enough, but he could not recall putting them on.

He shook his head in near disregard of yet another puzzle. Answers eluded him, but his situation still failed to lead to any true dismay.

The silence of the room, however, remained clearly evident. He could perceive nothing—not a hum of any motor in the distance, and no buzz from some electrical equipment. There was no rushing sound of water in some pipe, nor the whistle of a breeze in the air. He could also not detect any sound beyond the room. There were no birds singing, no insects buzzing, and no dogs barking. Even the sound of the rain he remembered pounding against his roof could not be heard.

As if to check his hearing once more, he clicked his tongue against the roof of his mouth, and he heard the snapping sound clear enough. Again, no echo, and the expanse returned to absolute silence.

He knelt down and felt the ground. It was indeed smooth and hard against the palm of his hand. Patting it firmly, it did not give in any fashion. To him, it felt as solid as any granite surface. He had never seen such a floor before and he marveled at its purity. He could find no trace of dust or dirt that spoiled the clean white surface that stretched out around him.

Shaking his head again, he stood back up and inhaled deeply through his nose. He wondered if he might sense the strong odor of disinfectant or cleanser, but instead, he smelled nothing. The air was dry and as empty to him as everything else within this strange room.

After a few moments, however, he realized something new, something that finally elicited a response from within. He was not breathing. He never exhaled that long breath he took through his nostrils. It remained in his lungs, or at least so it seemed. He felt not the slightest need to release his breath, to exhale out the air he had taken in.

He stood for long moments, concentrating on his own state

of being. He, in fact, was neither exhaling nor inhaling, yet he felt no strain. His body should have been rebelling at this inaction. Still, he felt no pressure building in his chest or pain growing in his head. His vision remained clear and his thoughts unmolested by the lack of oxygen. He realized that such a thing was just not possible, or at least it shouldn't be. Holding his breath even just for a minute should have created obvious discomfort, but he felt nothing.

The indifference that held sway over his emotions finally loosened as this one sudden insight shook him to his core. Something was indeed very different, something about him, and it went well beyond this strange and barren room.

Standing even more still, he tried to sense his own heartbeat. He could not. He placed his hand upon his chest. Nothing. He felt for a pulse at his wrist and then at his neck. Again, nothing. No breathing and no pulse, and yet he could move about with ease.

The quiet about him now grew even stronger, for his own body was as silent as tranquil air trapped in a tightly capped jar. Without distraction, he puzzled now over more than just his surroundings. His very state of being came into question, and he could not wipe away the perception that something was not right . . . well, that wasn't quite an accurate description. He didn't feel as if something was wrong, but an instinct within him latched upon an understanding that something of great significance had occurred.

His thoughts turned over the limited possibilities. He was not breathing and his heart was not beating, or at least he could not sense either of these functions. He considered what might cause such a bizarre state of existence.

Am I dreaming? Steven wondered.

This thought held momentary promise. If somehow he had fallen asleep in his chair with book in hand, perhaps the last few moments he could remember were nothing more than a dream. The distant rumble, the darkness, the upheaval—all of it just a moderate nightmare that still held his consciousness. That would certainly be a plausible explanation.

In the past, he recalled deep, heavy sleeps where he ultimately gained awareness of his dream state. In these instances, however, he always woke quickly once he reached this moment of realization. If such were the case, he expected to awake at any instant and find himself back in his home. He tried to will himself awake, to remove this room from his view and return to the chair in his living room.

Still here.

Dreaming became less of a credible explanation.

He thought back to his last known memory, and again he recalled the lights failing and his trip to the kitchen. He remembered a momentary calamity and then even greater darkness, as if a blanket had been thrown over him. Considering these elements, he wondered if he perhaps fell in the dark and struck his head. If such were the case, he could be unconscious on his kitchen floor, or perhaps somewhere in a hospital bed.

As he carried the possibility further, he wondered if he might actually be in a coma and his consciousness trapped in a dormant body.

That would explain much, he thought.

This consideration, however, failed to elicit an emotional response—mostly because it felt more like a hollow excuse than a rational consideration of the truth. Indifference returned to him as he held to these thoughts. This state of being now felt cold and empty, as if he stepped into a bubble of nothingness and floated within it without purpose or direction.

So far, only one insight invoked any true sensation within his being, and that was when he realized he was not breathing and his heart was still. Once more, Steven took hold of these simple facts and bore deeper for greater meaning.

Dreaming was one thing, but this was something else entirely, something more. He could feel his body, but it was different. He believed he felt his own substance, but he also sensed a change. The body he knew was gone. There was no fatigue in standing, no restlessness in remaining still. He felt no hunger or thirst. He was neither cold nor hot. There was also a greater freedom in his movements as if every joint, every muscle, every fiber were all honed to a perfect state of being.

There was a hard truth in these thoughts, a truth that needed to be accepted. That is what resonated deep down in his soul. The indifference again bled out of his being, replaced by a deeper sense of understanding.

Steven realized he had a choice at that moment. He could brush these thoughts away and attempt to rationalize his circumstances based on his previous earthly existence, or he could expand the limits of his consciousness and allow for new possibilities. The former held safety and the familiarity of his previous life, but it also seemed poisoned with hollow consequences. If he would allow himself the chance to consider other possibilities, he knew the empty fog would lift, but he could not know what he might finally discover.

With little internal debate, Steven pressed aside the desire to return to the secure sense of his familiar past. He allowed his awareness to break through the boundaries of rational thinking and he took hold of things he knew to be true. He was not dreaming, and he was not in some coma. He was somewhere else. He was beyond his old body, his essence deposited into something similar, but something new and better nonetheless.

Enlightenment grew just as his indifference faded further away. Allowing his understanding of the situation to grow and bloom, he muttered two simple words.

"I died."

With that said, he heard something in the distance—footsteps coming toward him. He turned about and saw what appeared to be a middle-aged man in casual pants and a collared, short sleeve shirt walking toward him with a warm smile.

"Hello, Steven. My name is Cham and I'm here to welcome you."

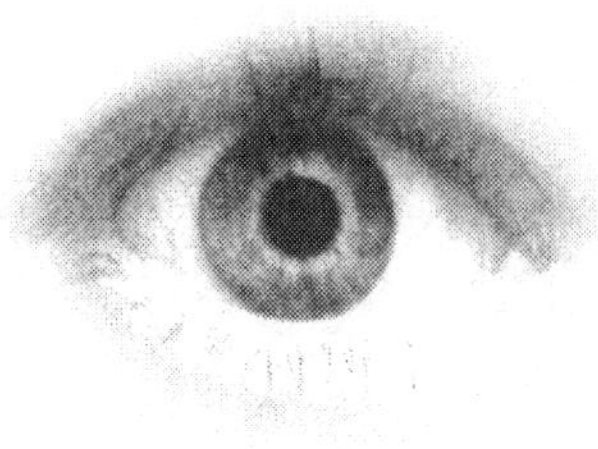

ASSISTANCE

Steven glanced quickly upon the newcomer, and at first said nothing. He did not recognize this person, this Cham, but he was already in a strange room, so why not have a stranger come visit? Steven's mind dwelled instead on much weightier considerations.

As he just professed aloud, he knew, in fact, that he had died. At least his body had died back on earth. The appearance of a stranger was hardly a great concern under such a revelation.

He did not yet know how he died, but it was no longer a question open for debate. He accepted this as cold, hard fact, and while he remained lucid in his thinking, he could not deny the oddities of his current situation.

Despite the clarity with which he accepted his death, his body seemed to be more or less intact. This created a paradox he could not solve. He could see, speak, hear, and even move about with ease. As he looked down upon his body, it appeared whole. He could find no sign of injury, no stain of blood, and no loss of flesh. This should have created some doubt in his mind about his demise, but none existed. There was nothing but simple acceptance of his mortal end.

Adding to the absurdity of his circumstance, he felt nothing like he might have imagined. There was no sorrow, no despair that shrouded his being. In fact, the acknowledgment of his death did little to raise even the slightest alarm. He faced his condition as more of a puzzle as opposed to some great tragedy. He was dead, and yet he did not seem to care.

Odd.

Looking at the stranger before him, Steven's almost surreal apathy—the indifference that held sway over any emotional outburst—remained strong, but not without total opposition. This time he held to a small but growing desire, a wish to understand his situation, and this craving eclipsed simple curiosity.

Steven had accepted the death of his human body based on his own rational considerations. No one guided him to this realization, no one informed him of his earthly demise. This came of his own perception, and he accepted this awareness with nothing more than his own strength of will. Still, even with this monumental recognition, he now remained determined to comprehend more of what he now faced, and this determination broke through the indifference that otherwise kept his emotions in check.

"Cham is it?" Steven asked to confirm the name of the person he did not recognize but now stood before him.

"Yes, it's Cham."

"That's an unusual name."

"Depends on how you look at it. My full name is actually Chamuel, but that's a bit too formal for me, so let's just keep it at Cham. And you are Steven."

"Yes, at least I was . . . I guess I still am." Steven nodded, accepting this as fact as well. He had not lost his identity, the consciousness of who he was. He might have died, but he was still Steven Drilach.

"You are still you, I assure you," the stranger confirmed.

Steven, however, knew that not all was the same as it was. He might have retained his identity, but he clearly understood that his surroundings and the scope of how he existed had changed dramatically.

"Well, I may be me, but I'm not the same as I was. Not completely. I know I died. I don't know exactly how it occurred, but something happened to me and now I'm here . . . wherever here is. This appears to be my body, but if I'm dead, I don't understand how I can even have a body." Steven shrugged at that thought, as if it was not all that important, and continued with what he observed. "I still seem to have arms and legs. I can feel things, and hear things, and I can talk to you as well. I'm not sure how I can accomplish that without breathing, but I can hear my voice, and it is my voice. I recognize it, and yet I don't understand how that's really possible. It all seems rather difficult to put together."

"I'm here to help you with that," Cham responded. "You sound like you have quite a few questions, where would you like to start?"

Steven looked into Cham's face. He still could not recognize this man.

"Do I know you?"

"No, we've never met."

"So you're not like a distant relative or a past friend or anything like that?"

"As I said, we've never met before."

"But you're here to help me?" Steven found this odd as well, and while he felt no true distrust or aversion to this stranger, he did not hide his skepticism. "Why?"

"Why not?" Cham responded confidently. "I knew you were here, and when you finally accepted what happened, I came in to help. Things work differently here. You don't have to call for help. It just shows up when you need it."

No further suspicion crossed Steven's mind, nor did any

gratitude. While he accepted Cham's answer at face value, he still wanted to understand this man better.

"You were sent here . . . to meet me here?"

"In a manner of speaking, yes, but it wasn't entirely my choice. You had to be open to it. I could have never entered this place if you didn't want me here."

"I'm not sure how I could have stopped you," Steven stated. "You seemed to appear on your own. It's not like I unlocked a door."

With that, Steven remembered the door embedded in the far wall to his left. He cast a quick glance in that direction. It remained closed, but as he inspected the door, he felt a wave of warmth flow over his being, almost as if he just pulled open an oven door where a pie had been baking on a cold winter's day. The door was important, not just to this room, but to him personally.

Cham called for Steven's attention once more as he continued his explanation. "You may not have physically unlocked a door, but you were certainly responsible for letting me in. I know you don't understand that, but we can get to that later. Let's just make sure you understand why I'm here and we can start answering some of your questions."

Steven took his focus from the door and turned it back upon Cham.

"How do you know I have questions about anything?" he wondered aloud.

"Everyone has questions when they first get here. Are you telling me you don't?"

Steven certainly had questions. In fact, curiosity proved to be the only stimulus within him. Not much else roused any reaction. He certainly faced no stirring emotions about his death. There was no denial, and no longing to return to an earthly life he now knew to be extinguished, but he could not dismiss his curiosity. "No, I have questions. I'm just wondering how you know."

"Hey, everybody dies at least once, so it's not like you're the first to come here like this. Questions are just part of the normal flow of things. That's one of the reasons I'm here. Think of me as your personal guide. I'm here specifically to assist you—to clear up some of the little details and allow you to feel more comfortable in your new surroundings."

Steven carefully considered this explanation. The stranger before him seemed sincere, and certainly questions did exist. A guide would be helpful under such circumstances, so why not?

"So I guess you're like my guardian angel."

At this, Cham shook his head. "No, nothing like that at all. That would imply that I somehow looked after you and guided you during your physical life, and that's just not true. You made your own decisions in life without guidance from me. I didn't really exist for you until you passed over to this new realm. I don't want you to get the wrong idea on that."

"So you don't know anything about me then? You don't know about my life, what I was like, what I did?"

"It's immaterial," Cham stated. "It's not like I kept watch on you while you were on earth and took notes on your activities."

"Really?"

"Absolutely."

This intrigued Steven. Offering help certainly seemed reasonable enough, but Cham's offer of personal guidance without knowing anything about Steven's life, especially under these circumstances, seemed almost inappropriate. It's one thing to help a complete stranger in the street, but this was *death*, the great beyond. Shouldn't his previous life have counted toward something here? Apparently, it did not, at least not as far as Cham was concerned. Steven questioned this openly.

"I would have thought it would have mattered what kind of person I was. It almost sounds like my life has nothing to do with what happens here."

"Your life on earth was your own. You did with it as you saw fit. I'm not here to judge you on that life. If anything, I'm here to assist you in making a smooth transition from that existence to this one."

"Then why would you automatically want to help me? What if I was the loner type and didn't want your help, or anyone's help for that matter? What if I liked to do things on my own?"

"How are you going to get any information if I leave you here alone?"

"I don't know, but it just surprises me you'd want to help me even though you don't know anything about me. I would also think you would want to be sure I deserved your assistance. What if I was a real bastard? What if I was a selfish con-artist that swindled elderly couples out of their life savings and left them to live in poverty?"

"Then you wouldn't be here," Cham answered as if Steven should have already known this. "If you weren't worth my assistance, you would never have made it to where you are now. But you are here, and because of that, I know I'm not wasting my time with you. You deserve to be here."

Steven looked about the place. It remained as it was when he first entered—a large empty room with plain white walls and very little of anything else. The only thing that appeared to have changed in the past few moments was the arrival of Cham.

"So rotten people don't end up here?" Steven asked as he gazed about the area. "I'll tell you the truth, this place doesn't look all that special. In fact, it looks pretty plain to me. You just made it sound as if this is some grand place that only good people get to see. I don't really see anything so spectacular about it."

"It may not be spectacular at the moment," Cham responded with a growing grin, "but it's better than where you would be if you were a selfish swindler of senior citizens, I can assure you of that."

The meaning of this statement was not lost on Steven.

"You mean those people go somewhere different?" He considered what that might mean and blurted out his surprise. "They go to hell . . . there is a hell?"

Cham's smile faded quickly. "I don't like to talk about that. It's not part of what I do. I'm here to help you with questions about what happened to you and where you go from here. You're not in hell, this is not hell, so there's no need talking about it."

This answer, though punctuated with a definite sense of finality on Cham's part, did not satisfy Steven, but he didn't quite know enough of his situation to press the issue. He was often cautious in his previous life and it seemed appropriate for him to remain so now. Discussing hell when you're dead is very much like harping on malpractice lawsuits right before a medical procedure. It just doesn't help the cause.

"Alright, this isn't hell. Is it heaven?" Steven asked.

"You could call it that."

That didn't inspire confidence in Steven, and the response certainly didn't satisfy him anymore than Cham's reply to the question regarding hell. This time, Steven decided to push for greater detail.

"I'm not sure what to call it," Steven acknowledged. He didn't know where he was. It wasn't hell, or so he was told, but did that necessarily make it heaven? He didn't want to jump to that conclusion. "That's why I asked you. Is it heaven or not?"

"Heaven is a rather subjective term."

"And hell isn't?"

"No, it's not," Cham responded firmly.

"We're not really getting anywhere," Steven suggested. Two questions asked about where he was, and still no firm answer.

"Actually, we are," Cham corrected Steven in an upbeat tone. "You realize and accept you're dead. That's a good thing. You now know you're not in hell. Believe me, that's a very good thing. That's pretty important progress if you ask me."

"Fine, that's progress, but that's not what I'm talking about. I asked you a question and you still haven't answered me. You said I could 'call' this place heaven. Well, I don't want to call it something it's not."

"And neither do I," Cham interrupted. "That's why I can't

answer your question as clearly as you would like. You want to know if this is heaven, but I can't say that for sure because I'm not sure what that would really mean to you. I'd rather you come to that conclusion on your own."

"So you won't tell me where I am?"

"I didn't say that. I'll tell you exactly where you are, but that's not what you asked. You asked if this was heaven, and for you, it might be. Who am I to say?"

"Okay, fine, why don't you tell me exactly where I am?"

"You're right here in front of me." Cham let out a short laugh. "Sorry, I know that was annoying, but you set yourself up for that."

"I suppose I did," Steven admitted. He would have sighed heavily, but since he wasn't breathing, sighing was no longer a natural response. Surprisingly, he also didn't feel anywhere near as frustrated as he believed he should. His feelings remained somehow in check, as if they were placed in neutral. Still, his curiosity had not faded and it pressed him onward.

"I won't ask exactly where I am, okay? But I would like to know what's going on here. If I really am dead, I assume I'm no longer on earth, is that correct?"

"That is completely true. You're not on earth. In fact, you're not at any particular position in that physical plane that we could use as a reference point. You are now in a different realm, a spiritual plane of existence that your previous body could never penetrate. Many people call this the afterlife, but that can be a confusing term. Look at how much confusion we created when we were talking about heaven and hell."

"And I'm still not certain where I am," Steven said with a bit more force.

Cham remained good-natured, if no less ambiguous. "The problem is this place really doesn't have a specific point of reference. I can't show it to you on a map. I mean, it's not like you were hurled through the galaxy and are now standing on some distant point in the universe. You're no longer in that universe . . . hey, that gives me an idea."

"What?" Steven asked with an expectant tone. Hearing that he was in the afterlife did not surprise him in any way, but it sounded as if Cham now found a way to make it clear exactly where he was, and Steven waited for this explanation intensely.

"This may work," Cham offered. "Think of outer space. Now take away all the planets, stars, asteroids, gases; take away all the debris, and that's kind of what you have here. No molecules, no elements, no physical substance as you used to understand it, just plain space. Now take that space and stretch it between the layers of the physical existence you once knew. No one can see it, it can't be touched, but it's still there. It's not quite an overlap because there are clear boundaries between the spiritual world and the physical world, but the two exist in coordination with each other."

"That means this place is just emptiness," Steven suggested as he tried to comprehend the meaning of Cham's words.

"It was, but not anymore. Now you're here to fill the emptiness. That's the difference between the blankness of outer space and what we have here. This area doesn't stay empty space. You're here now. You fill this space with your energy, but again, it's not just energy—it's consciousness, identity, and imagination. You project that throughout this space. The area is filled with the creativity of your thoughts. What you see here is of your own creation."

"So I created this big empty room?"

"Absolutely."

"Any idea why I would do that?" Steven asked as he glanced once more about the walls surrounding him. "Seems kind of strange I would make a big empty room."

"It's not strange at all," Cham replied. "In fact, it makes perfect sense to me. Your mind doesn't have a full grasp of what's happened to you yet, but the recesses of your consciousness guided by your spiritual awareness realize you have the power to shape the area around you. Your mind chose something safe, but also something simple. You created a floor, walls, and a ceiling to give this space form. That way, you have a point of reference. The room, however, did not exist until you made it so. You altered the space to meet your own perspective and expectations. The more you become aware of what you can do here, the more elaborate you can make this space."

"So I created this room because it was simple and safe, but I have the ability to turn this place into something more? Something complex?"

"You're starting to understand."

"So if I wanted to, I could create a big mega-rollercoaster and I could ride on it over and over?"

Cham's smile grew broader. "I like the way you think. And yes, you're getting the idea. This place is somewhat like your own personal playground, your own amusement park. You can create whatever you want here, and once you're tired of it, you can make something new. You can pretty much make any setting or scene you can imagine. You can make anything."

Steven believed he understood, and this realization brought him to one quick assumption. He looked down at his hands as he posed a question that might confirm his conclusion. "What about my body? I know I'm dead, but I still have my body. Is this my doing?"

"You catch on quick," Cham confirmed. "Yes, you created your body just as you created this room around you. Your body is long gone, dead and buried, or dead and burned if you preferred cremation. It's your consciousness, identity, and energy—your spirit if you like—that lives on. That is what is filling this space. You have, however, grown accustomed to having a body. In order for you to remain at ease with your surroundings, you simply recreated your body to establish your presence here."

"What about my clothes? These are different clothes than I wore last."

"Well, it's not like you went to some dresser drawer and

changed when you died. The truth is that you created them just as you created your body. Perhaps in the back of your mind, you always found these clothes to be very comfortable."

"I suppose I did." Steven paused and considered what he just learned more deeply. This body was no longer his true form. He was now a spirit, or so Cham claimed. And if so, he imagined he would have a more ghostly form. He spoke openly as he gauged his own thoughts. "If I created this body, then this isn't really how I look anymore. This is just an illusion. How can I see what I really look like?"

"Well, first of all, it's not really an illusion. You recreated your body in this space, so in this space it's very real."

"I'm not sure what that means, but even if it's real, it's still a creation of my own mind. It's like a covering for my true form. What if I want to know what my spirit looks like without this body I made?"

"That's kind of complicated to explain."

"Why?"

"Because at this moment you're still to some extent thinking the way you thought when you used to be alive with a mortal body. Didn't you hear what you just asked? You want to know what your spirit *looks* like. That implies seeing things with your eyes. You don't have eyes any more."

"But I can see you."

"Yes you can, but you perceive me as your mind wants to perceive me. I can tell you that what you *see* and what I *perceive* are two very different things."

"So you see me as something different? Do you see this room as something different?"

"No, I see what you created, but I can also see beyond that. Actually, 'see' isn't the best word. As I said, we don't have eyes anymore. It's more like being aware of something. In a spiritual world, you have the ability to perceive things that don't require physical attributes. You don't need sound waves to hear things or light to see things. Your perception is based on spiritual awareness, and this awareness will grow for you over time."

"I'm not sure if I'm following you on this," Steven admitted. Again, he felt no frustration, but Cham's explanations lacked a sense of clarity, as if the words were all there but the meaning was somehow hidden behind a fog. Steven realized he didn't have eyes, but he could still look around. It might not have been *seeing* things as he experienced when he had actual eyes, but the way in which he perceived the imagery around him seemed identical in practice.

Cham offered some solace. "Like I said, give it time. You need to adjust to everything that is here and there's a great deal around you that you haven't even experienced yet. Part of you has to let go of the old ways. That's not going to happen the first instant you're here. There's really no other way I can say it."

For the most part, Steven accepted the notion that he needed patience, but he also remained steadfast in his desire to understand as much as he could. He decided that he was not getting as clear a picture as he hoped, and he pressed for a new direction. "Look, I'm not sure I understand things any better than when I first got here. All I can figure out is that I created a body for my spirit and then an empty room for that body, but in truth, I don't really know where I am or how I got here."

"You seem to be a bit of a pessimist," Cham said. "You keep looking at the things you don't know, and you're ignoring what you've learned in only a few short moments. Seems to me, you're making more progress than you're willing to give yourself credit for."

"I'm not sure I've made any progress at all," Steven admitted. The only thing he really knew was that he was dead, a consideration that seemed surprisingly unimportant. On earth, death is severe. It's the end of everything. He faced it now with less concern than if he had been given a simple parking ticket. The level of apathy regarding this acknowledgment simply did not meet the measure he would have expected.

Cham offered comforting advice. "Hey, I know what you're going through. It's not a mystery to me. I know what you're feeling, and what you're not feeling. But you have to understand, you're just at the very beginning."

"The beginning to what?" Steven asked.

Cham opened his arms and scanned the entire room. "The beginning of appreciating what's really possible here. Yes, you made this room, but that's just a sliver of what you can do. As you move forward, you're going to experience some amazing things, things that are going to astound you, and I'm here to help you discover all of that and more."

Steven decided to turn the conversation toward something more concrete. "You want to help? Okay let's first deal with how I got here. How did I die?"

"It was a flood," Cham answered without hesitation. "It destroyed your house while you were in it."

Steven recalled the mayhem in his kitchen, the last memory of his previous life. A flood made sense.

"My house is gone?"

"Yes, but you really don't need it anymore."

Steven realized that was certainly true, but try as he might, he could not recall the actual moment of his death.

"Did I drown?"

"No, you were basically crushed to death."

"I don't remember that."

"It was very sudden, very quick. You never even saw the water."

"Wait a minute," Steven declared as he recalled something earlier that Cham had stated. "I thought you said you knew nothing about me or my life. That's what you said when I asked if you were my guardian angel. If that's true, how do you know this?"

Cham showed no reservation in explaining this apparent contradiction. "Remember when I said I perceive things differently than you do, that I do more than just *see* things, that I am actually more aware of things? Even if I know nothing of your life, I still can see your death. Your death is the event that brings you here and this I can perceive. As you continue to grow, you'll start to understand what I'm talking about. Your awareness will deepen and you will perceive things on different levels as well."

"This is getting confusing again. We seem to keep returning to this point, no matter what I do."

"That's only because you're still reacting as if you were back in your previous existence. Right now, for you, it's all about your comfort level. You've had a lifetime with your consciousness in a physical world. You had senses that you used to see, hear, smell, and feel things. That's what you're comfortable with, so you're still relying on those sensations to bring you information. The truth is, you don't have eyes, you don't have ears, and you don't have a nose. You are, however, aware of your surroundings. Your consciousness remains, but you perceive things on a different level. You don't have a true grasp of that yet, so you are falling back to what you used to know."

"And that's why I made this body," Steven stated as a greater understanding began to arise within him.

"Exactly. By doing so, you are more comfortable with this environment, but it also limits what you can perceive. Eventually, you will grow accustomed to your new surroundings and you will be able to perceive so much more. Think of yourself like a newborn back in the life you once knew. An infant has much to learn before it can truly appreciate all the things that the world has to offer. You are, in essence, facing the same circumstances as a newborn. You need to experience things here, which will allow you to grow, which will allow you to understand even more of what there is here in this new existence."

"Interesting," Steven allowed as he considered the analogy.

"Yes, it is."

Steven nodded and then considered another point that was nagging at him. "Let me go back to something else you said earlier. You said something about me accepting what happened. You showed up only after that. What did you mean by that?"

"You don't miss much. I'm impressed. As for what I meant, I meant exactly what I said. I could only show up when you accepted that you had died."

"You say that as if there was a chance you might not have showed up at all. Eventually, I had to accept what happened. That was really only a matter of time, right?"

"No. There are people that died a long time ago that have still not accepted they are dead."

"Really?"

"Definitely."

"What happens to them?"

"They become lost. Their consciousness clamps on to the old existence, never releasing it, but they have only the slimmest connection to it. They refuse to recognize this plane. They shun it and hold to what they used to know. Unfortunately, they become a shadow of themselves, a life with no true past and no future, only a present, and that life is meager at best."

"I understand that they wouldn't have a future, but why wouldn't they have a past? I remember my life, or at least most of it."

"But you remember all that you were, and keep it in context with your current state of being. Their past becomes clouded by what they can not accept. They return to a point in their lives and hold to it forever. They don't look back on their past as a way to experience some pleasant memory or to learn from some mistake. They lose what they were because they are no longer mortal, yet they attempt to walk a mortal world. Many of their memories fade as they can't reconcile their situation to what they are currently experiencing. Those that are caught in this state might hold to a few memories, maybe those that pertain to an event that kept them from accepting death. Those memories would represent all that they are, not what they were. They return to this past event and it becomes their current existence as they hold to it above all other things."

"Spirits can go back to earth, is that what you're saying?" Steven asked.

"Yes and no. They can't go back to the way things were, they have no physical properties left, and so they can't go back to their previous life. Still, there are links to that existence, links anyone can follow. These souls grab onto those links, take hold of them like lifelines and don't let go. Their entire existence becomes focused on that connection and they lose everything else. They retain a basic identity, but not the full composition of what they were because they are a spiritual energy holding onto a non-spiritual world."

"That could have happened to me?"

"It could happen to anyone that comes here. You faced a moment when you first arrived when you had to make a decision, you could have either accepted this new life or refused it. You know I'm telling you the truth on this, don't you?"

Steven recalled his own moment of acceptance. He knew the threat of refusing this new reality existed, and he remembered how hollow it felt.

"Yes," Steven admitted.

Cham pointed to the stairs that remained visible in the distance. "See those . . . those stairs? You made those when you made this room. You made them because when you first arrived in this realm, you still hadn't made that decision. You still did not accept your own death. Those stairs were your escape hatch, a way out."

"A way out to where?"

"Back to what you used to know. Like I said, there are links between this existence and the life you once led. If you could not accept your death, those stairs would have led back to the physical plane you once knew. They're not really stairs, but they represent links between the two planes. Connections between this realm and the physical world continue to exist, and you still have the ability to look into that old existence. The thing is if you did not accept your death, you would have been trapped between the two realms. Not a good thing."

Steven looked over to the stairs in the distance. "Where do they lead now?"

Cham shrugged at first. "They probably still lead back to earth, my guess would be somewhere that was important to you." Then he noticed Steven's growing interest. "I tell you what, why don't we take a look?"

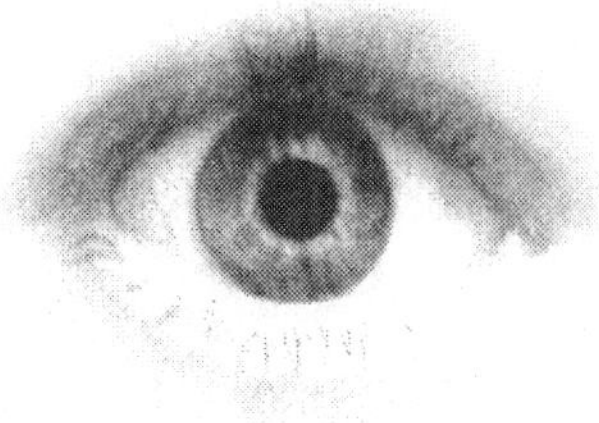

PAIN

"Where are we going to end up?" Steven wondered aloud as both he and Cham began to step toward the stairs several paces in front of them.

"I have no idea," Cham answered. "I didn't make the stairs, you did."

"Can they lead anywhere?"

"Sure. Time and space react differently here. There are connections that span the entire plane of physical existence."

"So we could end up on the moon, or even the other side of the universe?"

"It's possible, but not probable. Remember, you made these steps unconsciously. I would guess they lead back to something you knew. Have you been to the moon?"

Steven shook his head.

"No, I didn't think so," Cham continued, "so I'm betting against the moon. It could be anything out of your past—maybe something recent or maybe something from your childhood. There's no way to tell from here. It's not like we can check the mall directory, but there's one way to find out."

Cham paused as they reached the opening to the set of stairs that led downward. Several steps formed a casual, easy slope, and as they continued on beyond the line of sight, neither Steven nor Cham could see their ultimate destination. "You can go first, I can go first, or the steps are wide enough for us to walk down together, which do you prefer?"

"Let's take them side by side," Steven announced and then began a steady descent without waiting for further word from Cham.

Very quickly, Steven's head was below the floor of the room above him and still the steps went on down beyond his perception. Without knowing the end, he simply moved forward with growing curiosity. The walls remained plain white and clean on both sides. There were no hand rails, and his footfalls clapped out on the stone-like surface that was much like the floor of the room they departed.

Steven began to feel more than just a twinge of excitement. With the acceptance of his new surroundings came the realization that mysteries and revelations abounded at every turn. His spiritual countenance revealed his pleasure as he could not hide the grin that adorned his appearance. The slight pang of exhilaration grew quickly into a thrilling sense of new adventure as the indifference lifted from his soul. He knew he was returning to the world where he used to live, but he could not guess where he might end up. Like opening a surprise gift that was delivered by mail with no return address, he moved down the steps with an electric anticipation.

Suddenly, with one step, the stairwell simply vanished around him. He was no longer in that strange empty room, or on a staircase with no obvious destination. He was indeed back on earth, and back at a very familiar place.

It was near midday, for the sun shone brightly almost directly overhead in a serene blue, cloudless sky. The season had to be late spring for the trees were full with mature leaves that still held to that bright green hue of fresh growth. Only a very few blossoms remained on high branches—most were upon the ground, already faded or brown.

Despite the gorgeous clarity of the day, Steven's hope for adventure quickly returned to the dormancy that ruled his emotions with consistency since his passing. His previous excitement ebbed away to nothing as the disheartening appearance of his surroundings extinguished his previous enthusiasm.

To compound the dampening of his emotions, his lack of a physical connection to this world added to his indifference. He could not feel the warmth of the sun on his face to judge the temperature, even as it cast sharp shadows all around. He could not sense the force of the wind to say if it was warm from the south or cool from the north, but he knew it blew steady as it ruffled the leaves of the surrounding trees.

He looked upon a worn concrete slab that sat in the middle of a clearing. It remained covered in dirt and debris. Even as he recognized the general vicinity, very little was quite like he remembered. Trees and shrubs were missing, mud covered much of the grass, rubble was scattered across the area, and yet still he knew this was where his home once stood.

"I used to live here," he stated with a now expressionless face, his grin dissolved.

Steven turned about and looked up the shadow-covered country road. He scanned the surrounding woods. He didn't have many neighbors, none that lived close by anyway. He used to like it that way, liked the quiet. Now, however, it was beyond quiet to him. It was desperately lonely, forgotten, and abandoned.

With the suddenness of an unexpected detonation, Steven's emotions burst from their state of idleness. It was no longer excitement that flowed throughout his spirit. The emptiness within him shattered like icicles hitting cold, hard pavement as a pain struck him at his center. The emotion that took hold of him was nothing less than the most desperate grief he ever experienced.

Sorrow engulfed him giving no quarter, no mercy. He suddenly felt as if all hope had deserted him. The dreadful sensation grew to a point of bitter anguish. The dismay weighed on his center like a concrete block. He could not cry, and yet he felt if he did not release his sadness, he would drown in grief.

"What's happening to me," Steven begged of Cham. "I feel so sad, so awful. This is horrible! Why am I feeling this way?"

"Your home is gone." Cham answered with a hollow tone. There was no comfort in his voice, no compassion that Steven could take hold of for reassurance.

"I know it's gone! You told me it's gone, but why do I care so much?"

"Part of you is back on earth now. You're a spiritual presence in a physical world. You have not yet learned what that truly means, and so you have no control. Your emotions are torn between the two realms and they will react violently, sometimes angrily, sometimes painfully."

These words meant nothing to Steven. He retained the form of his previous body, even though that body no longer actually existed, and he could feel his emotions just as if he was experiencing severe physiological trauma. The pain swelled inside him, and he felt as if he would burst at any moment. Despite the fact he had no true legs, the shadow of his outline began to sway uncontrollably.

Such was the severity of his sorrow, his form collapsed to his knees, yet still he could not cry. There was no outlet for his anguish and it boiled like liquid in a covered pot. He could barely speak, but he found just enough strength to make a frantic plea.

"Make it stop, please make it stop!" It was a mere whisper as the pain flooded his ability to think, let alone speak.

"I can't," Cham answered.

With one colossal effort, Steven managed to blurt out one last appeal.

"Then help me out of here, we need to get out of here!"

"No," Cham stated with a firm grip on Steven's shoulder. "I can't help you, but it will pass. Give it time."

"I can't take it much longer!"

"Then it shouldn't last much longer."

Steven groaned and the shadowy image of his figure crumpled full on the ground. Cham's hand fell away from Steven's shoulder as Steven rolled over on his back to face the sky. It felt to him as if a giant was now stepping down upon him, crushing him with slow methodical pressure as opposed to one mighty stomp. At a point when Steven believed he could take no more, the pain exploded like a star going supernova, and then thankfully, stopped completely.

It seemed as if nothing remained inside Steven, as if all the pain and despair disintegrated in that ultimate explosion of grief. He felt like an empty casing, a hollow egg shell. Not even the slightest twinge of despair remained. There was only emptiness inside him.

Steven looked up to the sky, almost afraid to move, but greatly relieved to feel nothing at all once more. "It's gone, the pain is gone."

"I told you it would pass." Cham responded casually.

The silhouette of Steven's body slowly rose from the ground. His painful emotions had boiled over and out of his essence, at least for the moment. Everything he felt was now removed from his being. He staggered to his feet as he finally regained control over the full scope of his senses.

"What happened to me?" Steven demanded. "It felt so bad. I felt like I was back in my body again, but it was like being crushed."

"It's like I said," Cham explained, "you experienced the full effects of forcing your immortal soul into a physical world. Your emotions are no longer tuned to your old body, so you created a form that is similar. Bringing yourself to this physical world can set those emotions on fire as well as the form you created for yourself. You may not have a body anymore, but your emotions can make it seem like you do. They can create pain within you."

"I never felt that bad before, never!" Steven persisted.

"I don't doubt that for a minute because you've never been in this situation before. Connections may exist between the spiritual and physical planes, but never fool yourself, you no longer belong here. Certain events, certain places can play havoc with your essence here. Never forget that."

"But why did it happen here and now?"

It was Cham's turn to inspect the area. "Is it that surprising? This used to be your house . . . the slab is all that's left after the flood?"

Steven nodded in affirmation.

"Then this place was your home, your sanctuary. This was a place of safety for you," Cham said firmly. "It's gone now, and you're not here to rebuild. The link that your spiritual self is clinging to could not release the emotional tie you had to this place. I know I told you before your home was destroyed, but that was back on the spiritual plane of existence. You're here now to see it for yourself. Nothing I could have said could have prepared you for this. When you saw it like this, you could not control the outburst of pain. You no longer have a physical body, despite the fact it looks like you do. That's just an image you project. Without anything that acts as a true receptacle and a constraint for your spiritual essence, raw emotion will rage with little control."

"Am I going to experience pain like that again?"

"It is possible . . . almost a certainty, if we stay too long, but I believe that it's safe enough for us to look around for a while. When emotions explode like that, it will take some time for them to build up again, but it will happen."

"That means every time I come back to earth, I'm going to get hammered like that."

"Not exactly. There will come a time when you better understand the separation between the spiritual world and the physical world and you will gain greater control of your emotions. Still, that has not happened for you yet and that's why you don't wish to be trapped in this world. I said it before, you do not belong here."

"So this is what happens to people that don't accept death?"

"Believe me, it gets worse than this," Cham added. "Remember I said you unconsciously made those stairs as an escape back to this physical world?"

Steven nodded once more, "Yes."

"Obviously, your home is the strongest connection you have to this earth, but now it's gone. Imagine if you did not accept your death. You would want to return to this place, but your connection to this world is already dissolving before you. Eventually this place will change even more. It will become overgrown, swallowed by nature. Or perhaps someone will build a new house here. It won't be yours. You will have lost your anchor, and so you would also lose your past. Confusion and anger would most likely consume you, and there would be no future as well. There would be only hollow emptiness for you. Spirits trapped between both worlds can not find happiness in this state. Only when they accept their death do they have a chance to move on."

"Does that happen often? I mean, how many people choose not to accept their death?"

"It is very unusual, but think of the number of people that have lived on earth over the ages. Even if just a tiny fraction fail to accept their demise, imagine what number that would rise to over time. There are more here than anyone would like to believe."

"So there could be millions and millions of lost souls trapped here?"

"I wouldn't venture to guess at an actual number." Cham turned his head as if sniffing the wind. "A flood caused this disaster, which means there should be a river nearby, yes?"

Steven pointed over the trees up beyond the country road. "Yes, up that way."

"Let's go take a look. Rivers have been around for ages, much longer than roads. There's a good chance we might find one nearby."

The suggestion surprised Steven. "You want me to see one of these lost souls?"

"It will do you good to see one. That's part of the learning process. The more you experience, the greater your perception will grow."

"Are you sure we can find one?"

"Am I sure? No, not by any means, but as I said, rivers are good places to look. They served as roads before any car or cart was ever devised. There's a very good chance we will find someone that had a connection to the river that wouldn't accept his death. It won't take much time to check."

"That's good, because I don't want to stay here for long if I'm going to be hit by that sadness again. I'd rather not go through that ever again."

With that sentiment made clear, Steven began walking up the country road toward the river.

"Where are you going?" Cham asked.

"To the river. It's up this way." Steven nodded in the direction he moved but noticed Cham stood still. "Isn't that where you said we should go?"

"It is, but why are you walking?"

"How else are we going to get there?"

Cham said nothing, he simply looked upward.

A new wave of emotion, one with the power of great vibrancy, quickly rolled across Steven's essence as a question of delight burst in his mind. It went beyond a question, though he voiced it as one. It was a deep understanding, and one that generated exuberant expectations. There was no sorrow or pain as his emotions bubbled to life once more. This time, there was only joy.

"We can fly, can't we?"

"You already know the answer to that," Cham responded without reflecting any great excitement of his own.

"I do know . . . we can fly here. There's nothing to stop us."

Without another word, Steven sailed upward above the trees. His form came to a stop just above the tallest branches, and he floated in midair. He looked all about him, gazing over the land in every direction.

The view was beyond staggering, for he could see further and clearer than his old eyes would ever have allowed. The crispness of the images before him went beyond natural sight. It was almost like viewing the world through a floating telescope that could turn and focus instantly. If he so desired, he could count the veins in a leaf that hung upon a branch miles in the distance. He could see the soft folds of clouds far overhead and he knew he could reach them in an instant if he so desired.

Being freed of the constraints of a mortal body, his perception of the world was certainly enhanced, and it went beyond sight. He could hear everything he focused upon, all the while eliminating those sounds he found distracting. He could hear birds chirp and ignore the sounds of heavy traffic. When he turned his attention to a park far to the east, he could hear the laughs of children on a playground. The clarity was astounding.

As he turned about, the sense of sheer freedom that encompassed his being enthralled him. It was more than being a feather on the wind, more than a soaring bird flying over mountain tops. Gravity could not affect him. The wind meant nothing. He retained complete control over his position and he could move at will. He could remain aloft in the open air indefinitely. It required no energy on his part to stay above the ground. Beyond that, he could turn or glide about with the merest whisper of conscious thought.

Just as the first view of his destroyed home brought him despair, this ultimate sensation of freedom and near omnipotence delighted him beyond anything he had ever experienced.

Once more he felt like crying, but this time they would be tears of joy. He could not cry, but he cared little. He did not want this feeling to end. He embraced it, encouraged it to grow.

Steven began to soar about in large circles, then to dart up and down through the branches of the trees. When he first returned to the remnants of his home, he could not feel the wind, but he willed himself to sense it now. While he would not feel the slap of limbs against his face, he did feel the rush of air throughout his being.

Cham drifted up to meet him. He allowed Steven to soar about for long moments before he called out.

"I'm glad you're enjoying yourself, but don't get too caught up in this."

"Are you kidding?" Steven replied through a laugh as he encircled Cham in several flying twists and turns. "I don't think I could ever get tired of this."

"That may be true, but the more time you spend here, the more you leave yourself open to emotional outbursts that might not be so pleasant. Remember what you felt when you first arrived here. Your emotions can swing back in that direction without warning. You've had some fun, but let's move on quickly now."

With that warning, the joy Steven felt from flying left him like air from a burst balloon. He quickly disregarded his exaltation as he recalled the grief that brought him to his knees.

"You mean I can get hit by that feeling again . . . right out of the blue . . . even while flying around?"

"Absolutely. What if you spot something else around here that suddenly reminds you of some unhappy event? You'll focus on it and you could be overwhelmed in an instant. I know you were happy flying about, but you need to be careful. Sorry to bring that to an end, but you do have to remember where you are."

Steven shook his head, dissatisfied with the explanation. "This doesn't seem right. It's like swinging back and forth from happy to sad. Why am I feeling so much here?"

"Part of your question holds the answer to that. It's because you're here, here on earth and not back in the spiritual plane. There, patience is easy, it comes naturally. Here, it's not easy, and your emotions rule with haphazard dictation."

"What about you? Do you face the same problems?"

"My perception is different. I accept what I am, and know what I'm not. I could stay here for the passage of much time as defined by this world, and remain steady. The problem for you is that you have not yet defined your true essence. Complete perception as a spiritual being is not yet yours, and thus, you are much more susceptible. As your perception of your spiritual existence grows, you will be able to return here for extended visits and maintain much greater control, but that is in your future, and we must turn our attention to our present goals."

Steven remembered what they were looking for and pointed to the river. Even from high in the air and a fair distance away from its banks, he could hear the gurgling waters.

"The river's over there," he noted with a more somber tone. "I don't see anything special from here. What's the best way to go forward?"

Cham soared up closer to Steven's side and reviewed the surrounding landscape. "Let's follow it downstream for a while. We can get over the top of it and just continue following the current and see what we find."

As Steven now worried about the return of crushing sorrow, his elation over flying remained in check. He followed Cham over the treetops to the opening that allowed them to see the full width of the river. He glided silently for a while, simply staring down at the endless flow of water.

"What exactly are we looking for?" Steven finally broke the silence. "I mean, what should I look for? I see some people down there fishing, but they look like regular people. Are any of them dead?"

"No, they're all still alive so far."

"Would I be able to tell the difference?"

"The recently dead? Probably not. To you, they would look just like a regular person fishing, unless another fisherman sailed a boat through one. You'd probably notice that."

"Yeah, I guess I would. It's strange, though, to think there might be live people fishing with dead people. Kind of like those ghost stories you hear when you're a kid." That raised a new thought in Steven's mind. "Hey, is that how ghost stories get started? Is someone really seeing the dead?"

"Maybe," Cham replied as he appeared to be more concerned with scanning the banks of the river below. "Most stories are just that, stories. Still, it's not totally out of the question. Sometimes ghosts can be seen by just about anyone, but that's rare. Sometimes a specially gifted person can see the dead, but that's rarer still."

"So normally the dead that don't accept they're dead just walk around being ignored by everyone."

"That's pretty much how it works."

"And yet we're looking for them now. That seems odd."

Cham chuckled slightly. "Well remember, you're no longer just one of the mortals down there. Now, you can see both the living and the dead."

"But you said I wouldn't be able to tell the difference?"

"You probably won't. Take a look at me, take a look at yourself. If we weren't flying up in the air, could you see anything that makes us look different than the people down below us?"

"No, we pretty much look just like them."

"The recently dead are going to look like that, too. It's harder to pick them out."

"But you can?"

"Yes, I can. It's the same thing as being able to know how you died. I look and see beyond the physical attributes."

"What about the ones that aren't recently dead . . . the ones that have been dead for a while? What do they look like?"

Cham stopped and pointed down to the middle of the river. "They look like that."

Steven stopped gliding forward and came to a halt in midair directly over the river. He looked down upon the water and immediately spotted a faint disturbance. In one distinct location, the current appeared to bubble faster and the water broke in small waves as if some unseen hand redirected the surface. A dark gray mass, somewhat similar to a tiny storm cloud, sat in the middle of the flow. Although the near shapeless shadow appeared to rest half in and half out of the current, Steven could still distinguish the edges of the form that sat submerged in the dark water.

"Do you see her?" Cham asked.

"I see something, not sure what it is."

"It's a spirit."

"You said 'her', how do you know it's a *she*?"

"That's what she was in her previous life on earth. She was a female, so it's easier just to refer to her as such."

"How can you even tell she's a spirit, let alone that she was a woman when she used to be alive? It looks like a collection of mist to me."

"Stop trying to see things with just your perception of vision. In fact, don't try to *see* her at all. Simply try to comprehend her."

"I've no idea what you're talking about," Steven said.

"Okay, it's probably still a bit early for that. I see her as she was, as she wants to be, but can no longer be."

Steven tried to focus more closely on the gray cloud, but to no avail. Unlike Steven and Cham, each of whom retained a form similar to that of a human walking on earth, the shadowy figure was more of a gray haze, and lacked any real definition. He could see nothing of a woman in this shape, but accepted Cham's explanation.

"So that's a lost spirit, someone that can't accept being dead?"

"Yes. Take a good look. No true form, no future, no significant past. Just a collection of bitter emotions floating in a river."

"How long has she been here?"

"A very, very long time."

"How did she die?"

"She drowned in that river."

Almost as if the gray spirit suddenly heard the conversation and became enraged by it, the shadowy form flung itself airborne and departed the river bed like a missile locked upon a target. That target was Cham.

A high pitched shriek raged from the depths of the streaking silhouette as it sailed toward its intended victim with obvious malice. The misty spirit engulfed Cham with the full scope of its essence as if to choke him like smoke from a raging fire that would asphyxiate any helpless victim. It swirled around him, pulsating with anger just as the shrieks continued in intermittent shouts of fury.

Steven watched with a sense of wonder, never imagining he would see two spirits locked in some kind of pitched battle. He felt no desire to flee from the scene, for he felt no sense of danger, no threat to himself from the raging dead woman.

Still, he felt a need to offer his aid. He could not simply stand by and do nothing, and yet he had no idea what he might be able to do.

"Can I help?" he shouted. "What should I do?"

"There's no need for you to do anything," Cham replied as he calmly remained airborne and made no attempt to shake his attacker.

That would not do for Steven. A powerful sensation began to grow within him, and the need to lend assistance became so strong he believed he could almost touch it.

"I can't just float here and watch. Tell me how I can help."

"You're thinking like she thinks," Cham stated with near disregard to the being that engulfed him. "She thinks she's still alive, she thinks she can physically attack me. She can't hurt me. That's no longer possible for her."

The gray shadow shrieked even louder and swirled about Cham like a great tempest.

As her rage grew, Steven felt his own desires shift. He no

longer felt the need to assist Cham, but he felt an overwhelming yearning to save this woman from her torment. The need grew even more palpable than before and he could almost taste the necessity to offer aid.

He moved closer to the mass of gray, held out his arm, placed it within the swirling storm.

In a brief instant, he saw a woman at the front of a boat riding down the river. He felt unsteady, queasy in his stomach, as if he would be sick. Suddenly the world flipped about him, everything was upside down and then dark. He felt confusion and then denial.

Steven pulled his arm back from the gray mist, and the world came back into focus.

"You have to let go," Steven finally said. He did not know why he said those words. He knew so little of what was going on around him, and yet these are the words that came into his head. "There's nothing for you here."

The swirling ceased and the gray mist hung motionless in the air still surrounding Cham's form. If what was left of this woman held to any consciousness of her true circumstances, she would have beheld the sincerity within Steven. No such consciousness existed, however, and the form darted back to the river bed, back to the exact spot in which Steven first noticed her.

"And so she returns to the spot that holds her," Cham stated without any apparent compassion. "That is truly a lost soul, one that has never accepted her death and probably never will. Learn from that. If you ever allow your desire to return to this world to overtake your senses, remember what happens to those that can't let go."

Steven did not so easily release a different desire, a wish to help this poor soul. He looked down upon the small cloud within the water and wanted desperately to do something that might make a difference.

"Can we help her, make her understand?"

"Nothing we can do. Just look at her and realize that could have been you."

"Why did she attack you?"

"She sensed that I was here to help you, and I could only do that when you accepted your death. She never accepted her death, so I was an affront to her existence. I also don't think she liked me telling you how she died."

"Could she have been able to hurt you?"

"No, she's a spirit that thinks she's still alive. She thinks she has a mortal body. The truth is neither of us has a physical body. What could she have done?"

"I don't know. So much of this is still a mystery."

"Yes, but consider how much you've learned so far." Cham gave Steven a long look. "There's really nothing you can do to help her and it's time for us to get back."

Steven felt no reason to stay, save one. He knew he did not belong in this world anymore, but he found it difficult to simply turn his back on the woman in the river. He gave one last look to the dark mass and then turned his attention back to his guide.

"Nothing at all we can do for her?"

"Nothing," was Cham's flat response.

"Alright, let's get out of here. Time to move on." Steven then looked back towards where his house used to sit. Even at that distance, he could still see the slab. What he could not find was any trace of the steps that brought them both back to this world. "Don't we need to go back to those stairs?"

"Go back to them? You make it sound as if they physically exist back at your home. There are no real stairs. They are just a symbolic representation of the links between two planes of existence. You can make them appear anywhere when you really want."

"So what do I do, just click my heels and say something like *there's no place like home*?"

"You could if you want, but how about just focusing on leaving here and returning to where you belong. If you've really accepted your death, and I'm sure you have, you know how to make those stairs appear instinctively."

Steven considered the point, and deep in the recesses of his consciousness, he did know how to get back to where he belonged. He simply focused on the acceptance of his spiritual existence, and with that, a new staircase appeared just as the world around him became cloaked in a shroud of white mist.

Without a word, he placed his foot on the first apparent step. The mist dissolved and the clean white walls appeared on both sides. The stairs now stretched both upward before him and downward below him, and he could not see where they ended or began.

"Interesting," Steven remarked as a lull came over his spirit. He knew he was no longer in jeopardy of the severe emotional swings that plagued him when he ventured back upon the earth. His emotions fell under the calming grace of this new existence and he understood they would remain in control here.

Climbing the stairs, he soon saw them level off above him and lead to the plain white room that greeted him on his arrival. Upon reaching the flat floor, he stopped and looked back down from where he came.

"Will these stairs always lead back to what's left of my home?"

"They will lead wherever you want them to lead. Remember, they really aren't actual stairs. They just represent the connection back to the world you once knew. That connection will always exist for you here, so the symbol of the stairs will always remain. Where they go from here on in is up to you. You'll learn that very soon."

Steven thought of returning to earth at another time. At first, he considered the pain he felt upon reaching the tattered remnants of his previous home. He saw no reason to return, until he thought of the gray mist that marked what was left of some poor soul. He still wanted to help her, but in this place, the desire was not so urgent. Cham was right about that. Patience did come easy here.

Then Steven thought of flying, and for that, he might want to risk a return. "If I returned, what could happen? I mean is it possible it could still happen to me . . . that I could get trapped between the two realms?"

"I would like to say it's not, but I don't like to say anything is impossible here. Once you figure this place out, you'll see why."

If nothing is impossible, then anything is possible, Steven thought.

With that consideration, Steven's attention fell upon the closed door off against a far wall. Again, he felt great warmth fill his spirit, and in that moment, he needed to know what was behind it.

"What about the door?" he asked.

"I was wondering when you were going to ask about that."

"The door is important?"

"Yes, it is." Cham declared with a slight smile.

"Where does it lead?"

"That's the door that brings you to see God."

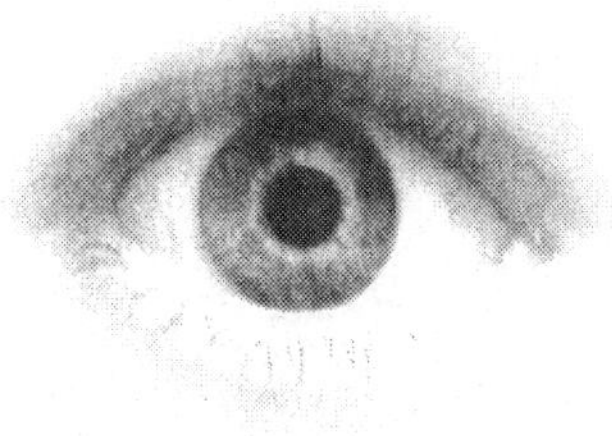

BARRIER

Once more, the indifference that filled Steven's essence began to lift like fog being burned off by the sun. As he focused more firmly on the closed door in the distance, an electric jubilation tingled throughout his being. No longer was he devoid of emotion. Instead, he felt a great joy bubble through his spirit. He could sense the room growing brighter, the walls and ceiling glowing with the sparkle of his own delight. The sensation became so strong it embraced him as if he had been hugged by a towering angel. He could barely speak his question, but he managed to whisper it loud enough for Cham to hear.

"God is behind that door?"

The moment of anticipation heightened to inconceivable levels. There was nothing he could imagine he would want to see more. The only thing that separated him from God was a single door. Steven felt his entire being swell with expectation. He would have dashed to the entrance in an instant had the overwhelming sense of importance not frozen him in place.

He could not know what to expect, what waited for him.

God, only a few steps away. The very thought seemed almost too profound to entertain in his mind.

"Behind *that* door?" Steven repeated.

"More or less," Cham answered. "The thing is . . . it's not really a door. The door is an image you are projecting, just like the stairs. You just made it that way so you could understand it better. The door represents the passageway from the space you occupy to God. The passage, or link, or connection, or whatever you wish to call it—it's a difficult concept to grasp. You needed to come up with something that would symbolize that pathway. I guess the image you felt most comfortable with was a door."

"I understand that," Steven said almost triumphantly. "It's like this room. The room is my way of giving substance to my surroundings, to allow me to place myself in perspective to what's around me. The door is the same thing, right?"

"Absolutely. You are indeed beginning to understand. And just so you know, creating a door is really not out of the ordinary. Fact is, a door makes perfect sense, but you could have created something else as well. A long spiraling staircase to another level would have made just as much sense, or a bridge over a river would have worked, too. Hey, I wouldn't have been surprised with a toll booth and a gate."

"But they all represent a kind of crossing from one place to another, don't they?"

"Yes, they do."

"Like I said, that makes sense to me," Steven admitted, "and all I have to do is walk over and turn the knob."

"Well . . . ." Cham paused for a long moment.

During that breath of time, Steven realized something very significant, something that slightly cut away at the inner feeling of elation that blazed within his being. A droplet of doubt splashed against his fire of exuberance, not enough to extinguish it, but enough to give him pause. And within that doubt, he sensed something in Cham's tone that made him ask a question of vital importance.

"Why is the door closed?"

"That's what I was about to point out," Cham replied. "It's closed because it's not quite time for you to meet with God."

This surprised Steven. More than just surprised him, it stunned him with a measure nearly equal to the joy he initially felt upon learning of God's close proximity. Even stunned could not fully describe the result of this revelation. Even though he no longer had a body, no longer had nerve endings that sent impulses to a brain that was not there, the disclosure reverberated through Steven's essence like a rolling tremor.

"Not time?" Steven responded with a tone that sounded more like a plea for mercy than a question of fact. "What do you mean?"

"I mean just what I said. You're not ready to see God."

"Not ready? Of course I'm ready. I've waited my whole life for this!"

"You waited a lifetime down on earth. You just got here. There are things you have to learn, things you have to figure out."

Confusion spread through Steven. He was so close to God, so close to coming face to face with an entity that for him represented the totality of goodness, and yet embraced so much mystery. The mystery of death had been lifted. He learned death was not the end of life, but the start of a new existence, an existence in an afterlife. Now that he was in that spiritual reality, how could he be barred from seeing God? It made no sense.

"You're telling me I'm not allowed to see God!" Steven exclaimed.

"I didn't say that," Cham responded with a calm demeanor. He spoke with a knowing and reassuring tone. "I said it wasn't *time* for you to meet God, not that you couldn't. The time will eventually come, you just have to wait for it."

Steven stood stone still. Cham's explanation quelled the growing pain within him but not completely. He found slight hope in these words, but he remained distraught in spirit. He could not understand why God would not see him.

"I'm dead, what else has to happen? What am I waiting for?"

Cham raised an eyebrow. "What? You think it's all up to you?"

"Who else is there?"

"How about God?" Cham pointed out.

Another sting of pain struck Steven's soul. Why would God shut him out? He focused on the door with all his being. He felt it pull to him even as it appeared so far away.

"Doesn't he want to see me?" Steven wondered aloud as if pleading to a judge after being convicted of some crime.

"Of course he does, but when you're ready. You're not going in to meet some blind date. We're talking about God. You just don't barge in. He invites you in."

"Isn't God supposed to help me learn things and figure them out?" Steven asked, grasping at anything that might bring him closer to a resolution to this growing dilemma.

"Yes, but there are certain things you have to take care of yourself."

"I thought that was what life was about," Steven declared in all honesty. He could not imagine why he was being separated from God. *Was he being punished for some colossal sin?*

"Did I do something wrong?"

"It's not so much about right and wrong. It's more about coming to a full understanding." Cham displayed a genuine concern towards Steven's growing dismay. "Don't get so upset. You have to understand . . . ."

Steven cut Cham off with a hissing rebuke that more than revealed the sting of rejection he felt. The emotions that ran loose through his system now contained more pain than joy, and it was that pain which he directed toward his guide. "Understand? What's there to understand?"

The door was no longer a symbol that marked a passageway to God. It was now a barrier, an obstruction that denied him access to where he wanted to go.

With the acknowledgment of such a discouraging revelation, Steven's soul sank. The glow of the room began to fade, and it appeared as if the walls began to close in upon them, all but the wall that held the single door. If anything, that wall seemed to pull away, as if it could never be reached no matter how fast Steven ran toward it.

Finally, Steven pulled his attention from the door and turned to Cham with a skeptical look of his own. Something felt very wrong about all of this. His pain turned over inside of him and it came out more as anger. It seemed beyond absurd that something as simple as a closed door could stand between him and God, especially in his current situation, a situation he made plain to Cham.

"But I died!"

"So?"

"So, isn't that what dying is supposed to be about?"

"Suddenly you're an expert?" Cham asked as he crossed his arms across his chest.

"What are you talking about?"

"I'm asking if you're an expert on death and dying."

"Of course not."

"Then why are you assuming that you instantly see God when you die?"

"I don't know. It just makes sense."

"How can it make sense?" Cham chuckled.

Steven did not like that laugh and a growing sense of discontent forged the will to defend himself. "It makes a heck of a lot more sense than some stupid closed door. People die and they see God, not some empty room. This isn't the way it's supposed to be."

"That's almost funny. By what rule of logic are you using to assume that would make sense? Did you read that in some handbook? Is there some kind of rule that I'm not aware of? What preconceived notion are you falling back upon that enables you to declare what makes sense and how things are supposed to be?"

Steven now looked back and forth from the door to Cham, his attention divided. It was not total confusion that swirled in his mind, but more of an uncertainty. He didn't know how to argue with Cham. Cham was his guide, here to help him. Still, this was God they were talking about. It was not some candy behind a glass window, and he was not some belligerent child demanding instant gratification. Something was indeed very wrong with what he was being told, but the words to define his growing misgivings eluded him.

"I don't know," Steven allowed, "but I've always assumed that when I died, I would meet God. It's not like I just made that up. And I can't believe that I'm the only one who thinks that way. Just about every religion I know of is based on the same concept."

"You're right, you're not the only one. Sure, people think they die, they go to heaven, they meet God and that's all there is to it. Well, I'm here to tell you there's more to it than that. Have you ever stopped to think about what heaven is really like?"

Steven did not know how to respond. He had previously asked if this place was heaven only to receive some cryptic response. Now, Cham was returning to the issue that was never really resolved.

"I don't know. . . ." Steven began, but his voice trailed off into obvious uncertainty.

"I'm serious about this, this is important," Cham persisted. "Have you ever thought about what heaven is really like?"

Steven felt as if he was being distracted, led away from the true point, but he managed to answer.

"I guess so. It's a good place, a place you wouldn't want to leave."

"And that's it?"

"What else do you want me to say?"

"So you thought heaven was just some city of gold? You enter the gates, say hello to God, and then what? Do you just sit around staring at the palace?"

"Why are you suddenly talking about heaven? I asked you

if this was heaven earlier, and you wouldn't answer me. I'm not sure where you're going with this," Steven admitted.

"Let me spell it out for you. We're talking about eternity. You have an existence now that spans forever. Do you have any idea what that means? We're no longer talking about hours and minutes, or weeks and months, or even years and centuries. Time is different here, but you still have to progress, and you do that by taking one step at a time and not worrying about how long things take. That's what you're worrying about now."

"I'm worrying about why God doesn't want to see me!"

"No, you're not. You're worrying about why God doesn't want to see you this very instant," Cham shot back. "This is a new existence for you, but there are some things you can compare to your old life. Just like back on earth, it's not all revealed to you on the day you're born. You grow, you experience things."

"So all those religions got it wrong?"

"I didn't say that."

"Then what are you saying?" Steven near demanded.

"I'm saying that you just got here. You might want to learn a few things before you start making assumptions. Remember I said you were like a newborn? Well, you're going to have to hold to that analogy for a while. Infants don't get to drive cars, they don't get married, they don't have offspring, heck they don't even tie their own shoes. Actually, it's quite a long list that infants are not able or allowed to do."

Steven was incredulous. "You're saying there are restrictions here?"

"You sound surprised?"

"I am . . . I don't know what to think anymore."

And this was very true as Steven now suffered from conflicting sensations. While he had lost the initial elation coursing through his being, he knew he could not simply dismiss the significance of being so near to God. He remained hopeful and expectant, thrilled at the opportunity to be so close to his

Creator. At the same time, the threat of disappointment and a festering doubt continued to feed a dull ache within him.

Cham simply smiled. "Well, that's just what it's like for a newborn. They lay there like a lump of jelly and look around wondering what everything is. They can't talk, they can't walk. All they can really do is eat, crap, sleep, and cry. Be thankful you can do a great deal more than that here, but that doesn't change the big picture."

Steven said nothing as he waited for further explanation as to what that might mean.

"You just got here," Cham continued. "I can't say exactly how long because time does work differently here, but that doesn't change the fact that you know very little about where you are and how things work around here. You have to learn a great deal, you have to experience certain things. Despite the fact that you've surprised me with just how far you have come, that doesn't mean you're ready for everything. Certain things are going to take time—meaning time here, not time as you understand it back from where you came from, so don't ask me how long it will take. The time it takes is based on your growth. You have to learn to crawl, then you learn to walk, then you learn to run, then you learn to leap. It's just that simple, and you shouldn't expect it to happen all at once the moment you get here."

"You're saying I have to wait?"

"That's exactly what I'm saying."

"What if I said I don't want to wait?"

"That would be understandable."

"Maybe to you, but I don't understand this at all. I've died, but I can't see God. What other kind of restrictions am I going to have to face?"

"Don't worry about those. The only one you have to worry about at the moment is that the door stays shut until God is ready to see you."

"Why don't I have to worry about the other restrictions?"

"Because you probably wouldn't understand them at this moment. If I told a two-year-old that he wasn't allowed to split an atom, do you think he'd understand what I was talking about?"

"I'm not sure I understand what you're talking about."

"Proves my point. Just be satisfied with the knowledge that there are not many restrictions here, and I'll fill you in as we go. As far as you're concerned, the only thing you have to accept is that the door is closed because you're not ready. It's as simple as that."

Steven, however, believed the explanation far from simple and was not quite ready to give up. He felt his initial delight drain out from his center. He did not enjoy feeling it dissipate, but he realized the doubt and disappointment also began to diminish as well. While he moved closer to his previous feelings of indifference, he had not forgotten the wave of happiness that seemed to emanate from the door in the distance.

"What do I have to do to be ready?" Steven asked with an obvious tinge of hope and expectation. "Do I have to pass some kind of test?"

"No, no test. You just have to keep growing, keep learning. God will know when it's time."

"So I just have to wait?"

Surprisingly, Cham chuckled again. "Don't make it sound like it will be so difficult. You have to realize where you are. Remember, patience no longer requires great effort. Deep inside you, you already know that. You started to feel it the moment you came here. Patience is the control of desires. It's easy to put your emotions in check here. You simply let the cares flow out of you and your worries are gone. It may seem harsh at first that you have to wait, but not if you realize the control you now have over such things as impatience. You don't have to feel anything if you don't want to. You know what I'm talking about, don't you?"

And Steven did understand this. He knew quite well that he felt very differently the moment he entered this place. Even at this moment, as he focused on Cham, Steven could take hold of a state near devoid of inner turmoil. All of the emotions that might pull at his consciousness faded out of his essence, and a controlled simplicity washed over his spirit.

"I think so," Steven admitted. "Ever since I've been here, there's not much that bothered me. I know I'm dead, but it doesn't concern me. I don't really know where I am, but I'm not worried about it. I don't feel cold, or hungry, or tired, so I'm not worried about any of that, either."

"Then stop worrying about the door," Cham added. "Cast it out of your mind just like everything else. Eventually when it's time, the door will open. Let it happen when it happens."

Steven looked at the door once more. As he did, he felt a strong energy pulse within him, a force that seemed so much more powerful than the indifference that allowed him to put his desires aside. This sensation threatened to obliterate his control and the urge to go to the door was very strong. More intriguing, he did not want to fight that urge, he wanted to take hold of it and sprint to the door as fast as he could.

Cham appeared to sense this and called for Steven's attention as he stepped between him and the door in the distance. "Be careful in what you do. Just like in your past life, there are certain temptations you need to stifle. If you keep focusing on that door, you're going to get yourself in trouble."

"What kind of trouble?" Steven wondered aloud as if only an afterthought. He almost didn't bother waiting for an answer. He was told God was behind that door. He believed that to be true, deep inside he knew it to be true. The indescribable joy he felt earlier began to rise once more, to course through his soul. He could not imagine what trouble could possibly exist in his urgency to see his Creator.

Cham, however, raised a concern that Steven could not ignore.

"Do not make a grave mistake, a mistake you would regret for a very, very long time. Just as in your previous life there are consequences to your actions here."

This warning gave Steven pause.

"Consequences? What kind of consequences could there be in wanting to see God?"

"It's no longer about just wanting to see God. This is more about barging in on God, placing your will above His. More than that, it's about you saying you know better than God. Not a good idea."

This consideration held more weight, and Steven's desire to ignore Cham diminished greatly. Steven didn't want to question God, but was that what he was really doing? How could he be sure? God wasn't telling him to keep the door closed, there wasn't a "Do Not Disturb" sign placed out for him to see. It was Cham that was telling him to wait. Was that acceptable?

"But how do I know God's will?" Steven asked. "Deep inside, it feels like I should open the door. I'm not talking about just *wanting* to do it, but I feel that I *should* do it. Do you understand? I don't want to insult you, but just because you tell me that I have to wait, I'm not sure if that's enough for me to accept."

"I'm not insulted, but let me point out that you don't have to just take my word for it. Remember, you are the one that made this room, and you also made that door. That means you're the one that made sure it was closed. Don't you think there's a good reason for that?"

This revelation truly did strike home. The door was closed when Steven first arrived in this place. That was beyond debate. It was shut before Cham even showed up. There was something to that, and Steven couldn't ignore it.

"Look," Cham continued, "there are some things you have to be careful of, some things you need to be mindful of. You made this room in a fashion that would make you feel as safe as possible. I'll prove that to you once you give me the chance to show you what you can do here. The closed door is just another safety device. You need that security because there are important things you need time to consider. Remember I told you that you weren't in hell? Well, just because you didn't get sent there immediately doesn't mean you won't end up there."

Steven cast his eyes from the door and upon the serious expression that now masked Cham's face.

"I'm not trying to scare you," Cham pressed. "You probably couldn't feel real fear here anyway. It doesn't exist for you in this place, but you do need to understand the importance of what I'm talking about."

"You're saying the consequences could be that severe if I make some kind of mistake?"

"Not a mistake, but a willful decision," Cham stated bluntly. "There's a big difference. And that decision, as I said, would deal with disregarding God's will. I told you the way it stands. You now know the situation. There would be no excuse, nothing to hide behind."

Steven thought of hell, wondered what it might be like. His focus was once more removed from the door as he considered his dilemma.

The thought of hell and total damnation did not truly frighten him, almost as if he believed such a fate was no longer truly possible for him. As Cham said, there was no fear in this place, but he remained cautious. He retained his cognitive abilities and his reasoning. He realized the door was shut and it had to be so for a reason. Perhaps caution was the smarter course of action in this matter.

Beyond that, he knew he could suppress his emotions. He could smother the desires within him, even the desire to see God. That was a lesson he understood. It was certainly more difficult than quelling his frustrations, but not impossible. Slowly the indifference that engulfed him upon his first arrival to this afterlife returned and washed away any pressing urges.

With his attention returned fully to Cham, Steven took hold of the one sentiment that remained prevalent within him. While he would remain cautious and patient, he would never fully relinquish his desire, *his need*, to pass through that door.

"I can't say I'm happy about this, but I will trust your guidance. I still want to get to the other side, and I want to do it as quickly as possible. Help me get there."

"That's what I'm here for," Cham offered. "You simply have to keep growing."

In that, Steven found something to grasp. He now had an objective beyond the door, but one that would eventually lead him to God. He would focus on that and hope it would lead him quickly to where he wanted to go.

"Okay, why don't you start sharing with me some of the things I can understand so I can start moving forward? You said you could show me how I created this room and what I can do here. Why don't we start there?"

"I would be delighted," Cham responded. A grin of his own formed on his lips as he prepared to explain what was now possible in this extraordinary realm. "This is where the fun begins. I'm going to show you all that you can do in this personal amusement park of yours. Get ready for a wild ride."

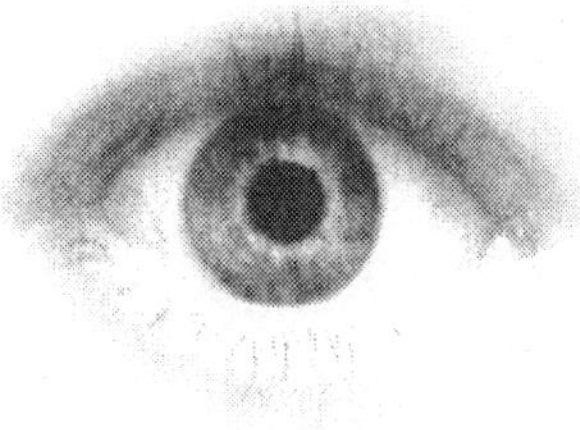

IMAGINATION

"Alright, here's the big secret about this place. I know I described it as empty space, but that's not really all it is. There's more to it than that, much more. What it really is, is a mirror of your imagination. Whatever your imagination can create will be conjured up before you. Just as you created this room, you can make anything your imagination can dream up. In fact, that's a good way to put it. Do you remember what it's like to dream while you were asleep?"

"Of course," Steven replied.

"Did you ever have some really great dreams, something you were sorry to wake up from?"

"Sure."

"Well, imagine having the power to create any dream you've ever had and experience it while you are totally awake. And it doesn't have to be some previous dream. It can be a totally new situation. It can be something that's familiar to you, or something you've never experienced before. Any dream, any fantasy, anything at all you can imagine—you have the power to create that right here."

Living a dream?

Creating fantasies?

This sounded almost too good to be true as Steven quickly considered the endless possibilities, but he wasn't sure he totally understood the implications. "Are you telling me that all I have to do is think up some dream or some fantasy and it will all play out right here?"

"That's exactly what I'm telling you. If you can dream it up, you can experience it. Any event, any object, any person; all you have to do is project it into your new surroundings. Whatever you create will be more real to you than the most vivid dream you ever previously experienced. The only limits placed on what happens here are the limits you place on yourself or the limits of your imagination."

"Really?"

Cham smiled broadly. "You have no idea! You might already have great expectations about what I just said, about creating your own dream and then experiencing it, but it goes far beyond that. There will be no fog of sleep, no sense of confusion that sometimes accompanies even the most vivid dream. You will be completely cognizant of your surroundings. It will actually be better than any dream you have had before."

"So I can pretend. . . ."

"Not pretend," Cham interrupted quickly. "It's not pretending. Remember you're not in the same place you used to be. You're still perceiving things in physical context, but it's not the same here. You think just because it's not a physical object, that it's not real. Here's a newsflash for you, there are no physical objects here. What you're dealing with now is something beyond that. This is your imagination, your creativity. What you make is your art and you get to experience it. It's difficult for you to grasp at this moment because you think if you imagine something, it's just make-believe. Right?"

"I guess."

"That guess would be wrong. What you create here is no

more make-believe than the paintings of great artists or the stories of great authors. They might not have had substance beyond the canvas or the page, they might have been abstract or fictional, but they became real enough to those that viewed them or read them. The images and concepts held substance in the minds of others, and so they went beyond just a passing thought in someone's mind. What is *real* is a different concept in this existence, but I assure you that you are not pretending."

Once more, Steven contemplated the prospect of bringing any dream to life. The dreams he recalled encompassed so many different situations, so many different experiences. If he could recreate them here, and expand upon them as well, he would not even know where to start.

"Okay, I'm not pretending, but are you saying I'm going to be able to create scenes, or situations, or—or whatever you want to call them—that could be as exotic as any dream I ever had?"

"That and so much more."

Steven pressed for greater confirmation. "And I will be fully awake, fully aware, as I experience these situations?"

"Indeed, I compared it to a dream only to give you a sense of what is possible. It is not like you will be in some daze and watching a projection of yourself. You will be totally immersed in the experience and completely able to make your own decisions, plan your own direction, and dictate your own actions. You won't be a spectator of an image of yourself. Instead, you will play the lead role."

"What about nightmares?" Steven interjected as he quickly considered the possible negative aspects in such an arrangement.

"That's a matter of perspective," Cham countered. "One person's nightmare might be another's favorite dream. I know that doesn't answer your question, but it needed to be said. Don't let that concern you because there is a distinction for you. You will not face anything you don't wish to face. You will not be placed in some horrible tragedy that you never wished to experience. In truth, there are no more nightmares for you. A true nightmare is having your fears thrust into your face and not being able to cope with them. That simply can not happen here. You will not find yourself in some unspeakable situation that will fill you with hopelessness, fear, and dread."

"So just good things," Steven offered.

"To a degree. If it had to be all good things, that would be a limitation, and there are almost no limitations. When I say there are no more nightmares for you, I'm not saying all your creations have to be happy moments of rainbows and unicorns. You can create anything you like, even if it's something that's frightening and dangerous. If you wish to challenge yourself here in conflicts that will test your bravery, you can. As I said, the only limits are the ones you place upon yourself."

The possibilities did indeed seem endless to Steven. If Cham was correct, he could create anything here. He just didn't know how to begin.

"Alright, I admit it sounds amazing, but how does it work?"

Cham smiled once more. "So you wish to get started?"

"Why not?"

"Excellent! It's not hard, it's not complicated, you just have to get the hang of it, and you're not going to do that until you get a true grip on where you are. To do that, you need to make your first step toward a greater awareness. There's nothing physical here, you're not a physical being. This is a spiritual world, so the substance of everything has nothing to do with material properties. Instead, it has everything to do with the interaction between what you are and what you perceive. I know it sounds confusing, but you have to stop thinking like you used to. You can experience things here, touch things here, feel things here, but it is not physical contact. It's spiritual contact."

Steven appeared a bit dazed by this explanation. It was not unexpected and Cham tried to make it clearer.

"When I say there is spiritual contact, I mean that is how you are interacting with your environment. You created this room, but you did so without consciously thinking about it.

You didn't shout out a command and you didn't build things from the ground up. It's not a puzzle you put together. Follow me so far?"

"Yes," Steven answered.

"You are, however, interacting with this room. The walls appear visible to you, you can walk on the floor, and as you have already seen, you can even descend the stairs in the distance. You are very much acting in a manner that is quite appropriate for you. So, even as we speak, you are already utilizing this space with your imagination. Right now, however, you are doing it indirectly, or perhaps subconsciously would be a better way to describe it. If you wanted to change this room, you could do so in an instant. You just have to allow your imagination the chance to create a new environment."

"So I could change how this room looks with a thought?"

"Absolutely, and to prove it, I want you to concentrate on a plain cardboard box. Create the image of that box in your mind, and then, place that image in the middle of the floor in front of us."

Without further questioning, Steven decided to simply follow Cham's instructions. He imagined a simple box made of brown shipping cardboard, the heavy corrugated kind that would almost cut off a limb if you received a paper cut from it.

Deep in his thoughts, he made the box fairly large. Not so big that it would overwhelm him, but large enough to hold something significant. He concentrated on a shape and size large enough to hold an ordinary kitchen appliance, removed any printing on the side, and held the image of that box in his mind.

Steven then focused on the center of the room, upon the clear white floor. On that very spot, he imagined the box in his thoughts would appear, and almost instantly, it did.

Feeling only mild surprise, Steven held out his hand and placed it on top of the box. Sure enough, the cardboard felt strong and sturdy. While he did not understand quite how he succeeded in making a box appear out of thin air, he knew the box came from his thoughts, came from his will.

He was connected to this space and more. The space was indeed a reflection of his imagination. The space was empty without him, but with him, he could fill it with whatever he chose. He sensed this. He then looked back to Cham with a sense of pride.

Cham simply nodded appreciatively.

"So all I have to do is think about things and they will appear?" Steven asked.

"Yes, but that's not the best way to have fun." Cham then spread his hands apart as he gazed about the room. "This space is a true receptacle of your imagination. In that way, its capabilities are almost limitless. It also means you don't have to concentrate specifically on an item to make it appear. I will use this room again as an example. You didn't have to purposely think about it to make it appear. You created this room immediately upon entering this space. You did so instinctively, without even knowing it. It was pulled from your thoughts without any effort on your part. In truth, forcing you to concentrate on everything you wanted to create would be way too constrictive. If you had to consciously focus on every small detail, you would probably go numb with the monotony. I just had you think of the box so we could get started. I wanted to show you the potential."

"How do I make things appear without thinking about them?" Steven pressed with curiosity.

"By understanding how to project your imagination. The box is an example of a forced projection. You consciously called for it. Your imagination doesn't have to be so restricted. Think of the dreams you had when you slept. You didn't specifically request them. They simply filled your thoughts from the inner reaches of your mind. They flowed from your imagination. That's what you have to do here. It's like turning on a faucet. You open up the spigot to let your imagination run free. It then fills this room with as much or as little direction as you allow."

"And I can do this?"

"Here you can, because here your essence fills this space and your imagination fills your essence. You couldn't do it back on a physical plane of existence because your body was the focal point in that realm. Not anymore, not here . . . here it is your spirit. Once you start working with it, you will immediately pick up on the sensation. It's like learning a language when you were a toddler. You picked up words, then made sentences, then started telling stories. No one really taught you how to do this; you just started doing it on your own. The same thing will happen here. The box was your first conscious word."

Steven looked at the box more carefully. He patted the sides and pushed at it slightly to see if it would move.

The box shook slightly, but then came to a rest. It felt solid enough, felt like heavy cardboard all around.

Cham allowed this inspection to go on for only a moment, and then continued with his explanation.

"The box may or may not be completely as you pictured it. It all depends on how much detail you allowed for it in your own mind. If you gave it dimensions in your mind, then it appears based on those instructions. Same thing for color, type of lid, whether it was open or closed, and so on. What you didn't actually consciously decide upon, your inner imagination filled in the gaps."

"So I just have to focus on basics and the details will all work themselves out?"

"That's one way to look at it. You really just have to let your imagination do the work on its own. When that happens, it's more of a flow of imagination than a projection of thought. That's the difference. It's almost as if you say where you want to go, and your imagination takes care of getting you there. When you truly start to trust your inner being, all kinds of things will flow from you freely. As I said before, it's like a faucet and you just have to turn on the spigot."

"I'm not sure I understand completely, but I think I have an idea of what you're talking about."

"And that's fine," Cham advised. "You don't need to get the whole thing at once, just keep moving forward. You're learning a new language and you can't expect to write a full novel on your first attempt."

Steven accepted that, but then returned his attention to the box before him. "I created this box, I thought about it, placed it in this spot in my mind, and now it's there. Does that mean it's just part of my imagination, a projection of my own mind?"

"It was, but now it's outside your imagination and here existing in this space. Don't let this create too much confusion for you. You'll run into a problem if you try to place the box in relative terms with your physical form. As I said, there are no true physical objects here, but I don't want you thinking that this box is an illusion. If you're asking if the box is part of you, or is it separate from you, then the answer is that it's both."

"How can it be both?"

"Because the box exists within this nonphysical space, but you fill up this space. The box is also in some ways independent of you. It's now outside of your imagination, but it's also within the space that you fill."

It was now Cham's turn to focus on the box. He smacked the side with an open hand. A loud slap rang out through the room.

"You see? I hit the box. You didn't imagine that, you didn't force that to happen. I created the action, but the box still reacted to it. The box is part of your imagination but it exists to respond to me as well. Got it?"

It was getting clearer to Steven. "Actually, yes I do!"

"That's good, because I don't know how else to explain it." Cham paused and then pointed to the box. "I want to see exactly how far you've come. This is a good way to test that. I'm going to open the box. What I want you to understand is that you have no idea what's in the box, got that?"

"You're right, I don't," Steven admitted.

"I'm serious," Cham said. "I don't want you consciously putting something in there. I want you to accept the fact that there's something in the box, but you have no idea what it is."

"I got it. I don't know."

"Then, let's give it a look."

With that said, Cham flipped open the top, and the room that had been silent and plain suddenly came to life in a vivid display of motion and color. A continuous and growing wave of birds flew out from the now open carton in a cackle of chirps and whistles. The roar of the flapping wings grew with each moment as dozens and dozens fluttered up into the open air in a mad dash to escape containment.

The flock consisted of birds Steven knew from his home. He saw robins and blue jays, cardinals and black birds, sparrows and crows, mourning doves and woodpeckers. The swarm of birds continued to flow from the box, far more than could possibly physically fit in that confined area, yet this seemed to hold no true limitation on what he witnessed. They became a giant, multicolored mass of fluttering feathers and their flight path created a streak of coordinated motion from the middle of the room to a second staircase off in the distance that led upward and out of sight.

Beyond the mayhem—the sights and sounds of furious upheaval—Steven realized the true meaning behind this display. This was, as Cham insisted, no simple illusion. In this place, within the boundaries of his essence, these birds truly existed. He could feel the breeze on his face from their flapping wings as certainly as he could see and hear their rush toward freedom.

What's more, Steven did not consciously place these birds in the carton. He might have influenced their appearance with the depths of his imagination, but he did not do so out of deliberate thought. He faced both astonishment and excitement from this insight for he understood what Cham meant about trusting his creativity and letting his own imagination spur on this surprise.

After long moments, the last of the birds finally exited the room. As the chaos diminished and a comforting silence returned, Steven carefully stepped closer and looked inside the brown cardboard container. It was now empty.

"Wow!" Steven finally said.

"Did that surprise you?" Cham asked with more than a hint of curiosity. It sounded as if he wanted confirmation more than anything else.

"I didn't expect that at all."

"Excellent. The truth of the matter is that you're accepting things faster than I anticipated."

"How's that?"

"Your imagination created those birds. Everything you saw came totally from within you. If you were truly surprised by that, it means you're already able to let your creativity do the work without any specific guidance. If you could surprise yourself with that, imagine what else is possible here?"

"I know," Steven admitted. "I was just thinking that. Those birds were really here. They came from me, and I understand that. But I didn't plan it. It just happened."

"You really are coming a long way fast."

That might have been true, and Steven could not deny the excitement he saw in the possibilities before him. He could not, however, completely disregard his own cautious nature. Even in spirit, he had to remain true to his character, and while he did not feel anxiety or nervousness, he considered all the possibilities and wondered about the extent of their influence.

"This may be a stupid question," Steven asked as he continued to inspect the empty box, "but what if those weren't birds?"

"What do you mean?" Cham responded.

"You said my imagination placed those birds in there. I believe that. Somehow I know it's true, but I also know I didn't consciously select the birds. It could have been anything that came out of there. It turned out to be birds and they just flew away, but what if it was something else? The size of the box didn't really matter. More birds came out then could have possibly fit, so anything could have come out. What if it was a bunch of lions and they decided to hang around?"

"What? You're worried you would have been eaten?"

"Well, actually . . . yes!" Then Steven corrected himself. "That's not quite right. It's not worry. It's not like I'm afraid of lions, which in itself sounds strange, so worry isn't the right word. But it seems to me if lions came out and they were as real as those birds, it might not be pleasant."

"You might need to reconsider your point of view on that. If you're worried what might have happened if they decided to turn you into the main course, you also have to remember that this isn't a physical world."

"So I can't be eaten by lions?"

"I didn't say that."

"You mean I can?!"

"If that's part of the scene your imagination plays out, then absolutely. I'm trying to tell you there are almost no limits here."

Steven quickly recalled the sensation of the birds so near to his face. He could see them, hear them, *feel* them. He did not want to imagine what it might feel like if it were lions trying to tear him apart.

"I think that might be a good limitation. 'Eaten by lions' is just not high on my to-do list," Steven stated, but for some reason, he felt no true alarm.

"Relax, you're still thinking like you're back in that old world of yours. Even if it was a bunch of lions and they ate you, you wouldn't die. You've already done that. You'd come right back here."

"I'm not sure I find that reassuring."

"You should," Cham stated. "It's like starting a game over. You lost the first time but you get to try again. Think of it this way, maybe it's your dream to be a circus performer, a lion-tamer. Maybe you'd want to take the easy route where there was never any risk of the lions turning on you. Then again, maybe you prefer the real threat of danger. For that to exist, the lions would have to be capable of attacking you, mauling you, perhaps even gobbling you up. It all depends on what you want."

"If lions attacked me, would it hurt?"

"It might. It all depends on how your imagination interacts with this new realm. Here, let me show you something. I'm going to punch you. I'm going to hit you right in the chin. It is not going to hurt you. In fact, you won't even feel it. You're just a spiritual being with no substance. If you have no substance, I can't really touch you. Ready?"

Steven shrugged. "Sure, why not."

Cham dropped his right arm to his side, made a fist, and swung a long looping hook towards Steven's jaw. His fist made impact just above Steven's chin, deflected off to the side, and then Cham's arm swung around to complete the follow through.

Steven felt nothing.

"You're right. I didn't feel it. Does that mean I'm not going to feel anything here? No . . . that's not true. I felt the birds. I could feel the wind they made. I thought you also said it might hurt if lions attacked me?"

"I'm not done," Cham stated firmly. "Now, I want you to consider what it would be like if I hit you back when you had a mortal body. Think about what it would feel like, where it would hurt, what might happen to you. Bring it all to life in your imagination. Don't just project the actions of me swinging at you in your mind. You have to also put emphasis on how it would feel—what would it be like to actually get hit in the jaw. Do you have a sense of that?"

"Sure, I guess so."

Without another word, Cham swung once more at Steven's jaw. The punch landed and this time Steven took a step back.

"Ow! That hurt!"

"You did that," Cham said without apology.

Steven, however, did not feel as if the fault fell upon him.

"What? What do you mean I did that? You're the one that swung at me."

"Yes, but you're the one that made it hurt. I did no real damage to you. You don't have a chin for me to hit. The results of my action were the byproduct of your imagination, not my fist. That's what I'm talking about with the lions. How it all feels is going to be up to you."

"This is supposed to make me happy? I can be hurt here . . . injured?"

"No, you can feel, but you can't be injured. That's what I'm trying to say. You haven't been injured. You have no true substance to bear that injury. You have no flesh to bruise and no bones to break. It's your imagination that brought the pain to life."

"I'm not sure I liked it, or that I'm going to like the thought of facing pain in the future."

"How much pain you feel is going to be totally up to you. You felt pain this time because I asked you to focus consciously on what it would feel like if I hit you. If you don't want to feel pain next time, simply imagine that it won't hurt, that you're invulnerable to pain. Problem solved."

"Why would anyone want to feel pain after they've died?"

"Remember what I told you about someone that might dream of being a lion tamer? Everyone has different desires, different dreams and fantasies. If someone wants to live out a dream of being a heavyweight boxer, maybe that person has to face the possibility of being hit and it actually hurting."

Steven could not argue with that logic, but he found no desire to experience being punched in the face.

"Alright, I'll accept that I can avoid pain if I want to, but I'd like to see how I can experience those things I would enjoy."

Cham displayed no reservation in aiding Steven toward that end. "What is it you'd like to try first?"

Steven seized upon a deep desire he had most of his life and he admitted to it without hesitation.

"I'd like to play music!"

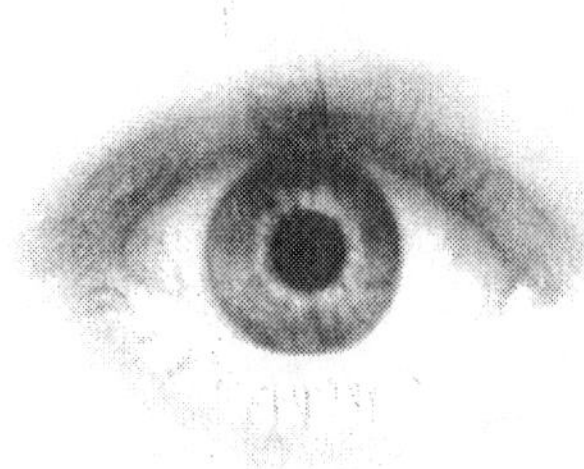

ASPIRATION

Steven reflected on the failed musical endeavors of his past life with a lighthearted chuckle. “I took lessons for a while when I was a kid. I learned to read music and I understood music theory. I reached a level where I could almost actually play something recognizable, but it was always a struggle. When I got older, I tried to teach myself on different instruments. I’d read books, watch videos, but I would always hit a wall. God, I must have played ‘Twinkle, Twinkle Little Star’ about ten thousand times on I don’t know how many different instruments.”

“What instruments did you try to play?” Cham asked.

“It would be easier to list those I didn’t try to play. I tried the guitar, the saxophone, the drums . . . I even tried the harmonica. I never had a real piano, but I bought one of those electric keyboards, the kind that can synthesize all different sounds. I still remember the guy in the showroom pushing a few buttons and then playing some song like he was accompanied by about twelve different instruments. He smiled and laughed as he played without looking, and he assured me the thing would do almost all the work. All I had to do was follow along with the little lights that would tell me what keys to press. I got home and tried following along and I couldn't do anything with it. I might as well have been a three year old banging away on a pot with a wooden spoon. Man, it was sad."

Almost mournfully, Steven thought back on all the times he attempted to create music. Like walking past gravestones of far removed relatives, his memories dipped into the shallow relationship with each instrument. He never developed a true bond with any of them, despite his deep desire.

He wanted so badly to be able to play, to fill the void with the grand and triumphant sound of joyous and powerful music. He loved listening to songs of all type, but he wanted more. He wanted it to come from him, not from the radio or from some electronic device. Despite his failings, he never lost that desire or his love of music.

"And you never learned to play any of those instruments?" Cham asked.

"Like I said, eventually I was able to play a little, if you could really call it that. Like all those kiddy songs you first learn to play, but I tell you, it never sounded really good. It was halting, stumbling, always with a bad note here or there. God, it was awful."

"Awful to you, or awful for anybody? Some people have high expectations of themselves and when they aren't the absolute best, they consider themselves terrible. You're not a perfectionist are you?"

"No, I can honestly say I would have gladly accepted several levels below perfect. Heck, I would have accepted several levels below average. What I was able to play wasn't really even music. It was a bad recital of a simplistic song that could drive a sane person mad. I was just plain awful."

"So you gave an effort, but it never panned out?"

"That about sums it up. I just couldn't get my hands, or my fingers to do what they needed to do on their own. I had no instinct for it, no inherent ability. It was like I had to force every move. Nothing came naturally. You have no idea how frustrating that was."

Steven laughed again at his own musical ineptitude, but despite his good nature, it still hurt. For him, it was failure—total and complete.

He held his left hand out to the side and he started to strum his right hand in front of him like he was playing guitar. He looked back and forth from one hand to the other as he continued explaining his lack of skill.

"If I was able to get one hand to do the right thing, the other hand would do something wrong. Then I'd change my focus to that hand, and the other hand would mess up. If by some miracle I got both hands in the right place, my timing would be off. Music has to have rhythm. When it's off, it's obvious. It was so bad even I didn't like listening to it, and I was the one playing. Do you know how bad that has to be?"

"I can take a guess."

"I'm sure you can. I know I'm not alone. There's a bunch of people I knew that could never play. They were tone deaf or just didn't have any rhythm, just no gift at music at all. And that's the truth, I've always thought of it as a gift. You either have it or you don't. And I make no bones about it. I don't. Like I said, I could learn a bit, make a bit of progress, and then that was it. No matter how long I practiced, I couldn't get any better. It wasn't that I didn't try, or didn't want to. I just don't have it in me. You know what I'm saying?"

Cham nodded. "I agree with you. Many talents are a gift. Musical talent is one of them."

Steven would not dispute that as he continued to offer his own experiences from the life he used to know. "You know what really irritated me? While music never came naturally for me, I would come across other people that never took a lesson in their life and they could pick up an instrument and just start to play. Do you know how frustrating that is? I try for years and years and all I could do is stumble through 'Mary had a Little Lamb' and these people sit down at a piano and start playing a song on the radio as if it were nothing. They didn't read music, they didn't even know how. They just did it by ear."

"I could see where that would be frustrating."

"Tell me about it. To make it worse, they acted like it was no big deal, like they could do it in their sleep and it really wasn't all that exciting. I wanted to scream."

"Some people never understand their own talents," Cham offered. "It takes someone that lacks the talent to point out how special it is."

"Boy, ain't that the truth. I had to focus, I mean literally concentrate fully on every movement and on every last note. Then I'd watch someone that didn't have to think about it at all. It was like breathing to them. They'd just pick up a guitar and start to play, or sit down in front of a set of drums and wail away. It would sound great and they just shrugged like there was nothing to it. I'd try to explain how hard it was for me to do what they could do naturally. I don't think they realized how gifted they were, even after I explained it to them."

Cham empathized, but he also now offered a ray of hope. His words rang out with an almost musical lilt. "I'm sorry you could never be as good as you wanted. That doesn't mean you have to accept that now. What you could not have back on earth is often well within your reach here. Back there, you had to rely on your physical gifts and talents, but things are different here."

Steven felt a surge of excitement, almost to the same degree as when he learned he could fly back on earth.

Was this really true? Could he really make music here?

He thought of his past attempts at trying to play some instrument.

Could that all change?

He did not, however, know for sure what he could actually do in this place, and he immediately tempered his expectations to avoid disappointment. He had been through that before.

"How are they different?"

"The obvious difference is that you direct what happens here," Cham stated. "Remember what I said before, it's your imagination and creativity that fills this space. If you can imagine it, you can create it."

Skepticism quickly followed Steven's moment of hope, and the memories of musical failure forced any expectations aside. "I was able to imagine playing musical instruments quite well back when I was alive on earth. That didn't translate into any successful experiences."

"But you're no longer back on earth."

Steven could not argue that particular point. This was certainly not earth, but he was still Steven Drilach. He knew that had not changed. "True, but like I said, I believe it took natural talent. I didn't possess it then, and I'm not sure I possess it now. I mean, I admit some things are different here but I also think I'm still the same person I always was. It's hard for me to believe that I've suddenly gained some new talent."

"You're right. You are still very much the same person. Your character, your identity, these things remain, as do much of your interests. You were interested in playing music before, and it's clear that this interest remains with you now."

"Well then, wouldn't my talents be the same as well, or rather the lack of talent?"

"Not necessarily, that's a different concept."

"Different? How?"

"When you think of certain skills and talents that applied to a mortal life, you'd be surprised how many are based on physical ability." Cham held up his index finger to make a clear point. "The important consideration is that this is no longer a constraint. The basis of your talent now is only limited by your imagination. Maybe you could not run very fast back in your previous life. Here, if you can imagine running as fast as lightning, you can. Maybe you always wanted to dance, but your body lacked the coordination. Here, you can dance like walking on clouds, if you can imagine it. The same goes for playing music."

Steven found this concept difficult to believe, much more difficult than altering the space around him. Creating a box out of thin air or even having it filled beyond capacity with numerous birds was one thing. If he accepted that he manipulated his surroundings with his imagination, then he could acknowledge the removal of certain restrictions. Changing what he was or even just changing some of his abilities, however, well that was something else, and he continued to voice his doubts.

"That's all there is to it? I find that almost impossible to believe."

"You shouldn't. This space echoes your thoughts. It's not like you need to have the physical gift to play music. You don't have to teach your fingers which string to pluck on a guitar or which key to strike on a piano. There are no strings, there are no piano keys. You don't have fingers. What you have to do is let your imagination create the song, or recreate it if you want to play one from memory. It is that power that creates the music here, not the physical talents that translate into the motion of a hand or finger."

Steven remained doubtful, almost as if he would not allow himself to accept this possibility. He had been stung by bitter disappointment before, picking up a new instrument and vowing this time it would be different. He always made a valiant effort, and yet each time his ultimate goal remained out of reach.

Cham sensed the doubt. "You really don't believe me do you?"

"I want to. I really do, you have no idea, but you have to understand, I spent so many years trying to learn. It just never worked out. That's a hard thing to forget."

Cham urged him to drop his reservations. "I don't want to push anything on you, but there is something you need to understand. If you want this to work, you have to believe in it. Whatever happens here, comes from you. If you won't accept it as being possible, then it probably won't happen."

The doubt within Steven suddenly grew stronger and now he felt almost vindicated for remaining cautious. "Now you're saying I won't be able to play?"

"I'm saying you're stopping yourself. If you put a roadblock up on your own imagination, how are you going to get through that?"

"Well, I'm sorry, but it's hard for me to just forget all those years of trying and never succeeding."

"That was your old life. Listen, you said you had to force everything when you taught yourself how to play an instrument. What is it you had to force? It was your body. It might have been your hands or your feet. Maybe you just lacked the coordination to do everything at once. Don't you see? Those are physical limitations. They don't apply here."

"I can accept that," Steven conceded, "but how do I play a musical instrument without thinking about using some part of my body, even if it's not my real body?"

"Do you think musical artists write songs with their hands? They write them in their heads. They write them with their creativity. That's all you have to do here. Let the sound flow out from inside you. Don't put the illusion of a body in the way."

Steven just shook his head.

If Cham felt frustration with Steven's reluctance, he did not show it. He plowed ahead, determined to make his point, to convince Steven that his concerns were unfounded. "I want you to try something. Don't worry about arguing with me. We'll just accept you don't have a natural talent for music. That's not what I want to do anymore. Instead, think of a song, any song, just think of it in your mind. Don't hum it or try to sing it. Just let it run through your thoughts. I know you can do that."

Steven did as he was told. He thought of a song he heard as a kid, a song he always loved. It was called "In the Mood" and it always made him happy. It was swing. There were no vocals, so there were no words. The tune grew slowly but forcefully in his mind as he imagined the saxophones, trumpets and trombones of a big band orchestra blaring out the melodies and harmonies. He nodded to the imaginary rhythm as he imagined the beat of the drums and the strum of the bass fiddle.

"Now, don't think of anything else," Cham instructed, "don't try to analyze it any further. Just let it out, project it as if you wanted the song in your mind to be heard by people all the way back to earth. Just let it out now!"

Steven had no idea how it happened but the room suddenly came to life with the song that had been playing in his mind. It obliterated the silence and music came from everywhere at once, and what a triumphant sound it was!

There were no halting, stumbling, ill-timed notes struck out one at a time from unsteady fingers. It was not the pitiful sound that he was accustomed to hearing come from a guitar in his hands, a drum set around his knees, or a saxophone at his lips. This was a full arrangement of a pure big band orchestra and it was both beautiful and powerful.

At first, Steven could not believe what he was hearing. It sounded much too good to be true. Unwilling to accept what he heard, or perhaps unwilling to believe that he had anything to do with the music filling the space around him, his mind went into a dead stop. He called for an immediate halt, and the room fell into silence once more.

Cham waited, as if wondering whether Steven was going to begin again or suddenly change songs. When the still quiet remained, he pressed the issue at hand.

"Why did you stop?"

"I stopped because it wasn't right."

"What wasn't right? It sounded great to me."

"I know it sounded great, but that's not what I want to do, it's not what I was talking about at all. I want the music to come from me. I don't want to be mimicking someone else."

"You don't think that music came from you?"

"I wasn't playing anything," Steven quipped. "All I was doing was thinking about what I've already heard someone else do. I don't want to just replay some recording I've listened to before. If that's the case, I'm just a piece of equipment. There are all kinds of devices that can play back music. That's not what I want to do."

"And it's not what you *are* doing!" Cham responded. "That music did come from you, and I can prove it. Think of a drum set and place it in front of you just like you did with the box. Do it now, don't argue about anything else, just do it."

"Fine," Steven agreed passively. With a single thought, a drum set suddenly appeared before him.

"Grab the sticks and sit down."

Again, Steven simply followed orders, picked up the drumsticks and sat down on the stool behind the bass drum.

Cham gave yet another quick order. "Now, project the music again, just like you did last time, don't try to consider where it's coming from, just do it."

The swinging sound of "In the Mood" immediately rang out once more through the room.

"Now, play the drums, but not with anxiety. Don't think about how you have to move your hands or feet, just think about the beat in the song. It's like playing air guitar but with drums. Don't think beyond that, just try it."

Steven started tapping his feet upon the pedals and swinging his arms around the drums. The beat in the room switched and it now matched his very movements. The sound also came clearly from the drums in front of him as opposed to some unknown place in the distance.

Cham would not let Steven stop to consider what was happening. He urged him on. "Don't think about what you have to do next! Don't think about where you have to strike, just project the music out of you like you're doing. Let your imagination create the music and then let your own form follow that lead, not the other way around. Your arms will move naturally because you really don't have a body anymore, but you can match your movements to the music in your head."

Steven followed the commands. He focused on the music in his thoughts. He simply let it pour out of him, and the form of his body followed as he struck the drums before him in perfect synchronization.

"You're not done," Cham persisted. "Change the instruments in your mind. Stop using trumpets and trombones. Make it something else, whatever you want."

Steven kept the melody and harmony clear in his thoughts but he changed the sound from the instruments in a big band orchestra to a string orchestra. The sounds of saxophones were replaced by violas, trumpets by violins, and trombones by cellos. At first, the music seemed odd and out of tune, but slowly it became crisper and cleaner.

"You control the tempo, pick it up, make it faster," Cham urged Steven on.

Steven did so and his hands and feet moved faster and the pace of the song quickened at the command of his own movements.

"Do you see?" Cham shouted over the growing crescendo. "You're not replaying anything! You're no piece of electronic equipment simply replaying some recording imprinted in your memory. The music changes at your command, your creativity changed the very sound and your will changes the very pace. You are playing those drums as naturally and as instinctively as anyone born with the intrinsic talent to do so."

Steven knew it was true. Finally, he was making music. He could change the rhythm at will. His imagination powered his movements and his movements created the beat. Even the accompanying instruments came from within him and he could alter their sounds as well. He kept the stringed instruments in his mind as he brought back the big band orchestra. As the trumpets, saxophones and trombones returned, the song strengthened with amazing power.

He could not believe what he was doing. He was actually playing a song, keeping beat, filling an arrangement. Every sound was coming from him and he controlled them all. He added new sounds, removed others. He kept wailing away on the drums all the while maintaining perfect rhythm, or making variations as he saw fit. He didn't have to think about what drum to strike or which hand to move, or how to tap his foot. His imagination kept everything in sync, and Steven knew without doubt that he made this music, no one else.

For one brief glorious moment, he felt an elation that matched the thrill of flying he felt earlier. This was a dream come true, a dream he once thought completely out of his reach, but no more. There was no more failure, no more disappointment. He could do what he always wanted to do and it felt greater than victory. It felt like paradise. The jubilation exploded at his core and the music around him grew in intensity. The sound was so vibrant, so alive, and he played the drums as he always wished to, as if it came naturally, as if he had been born with that great gift.

At that same instant, he looked upon the closed door in the distance. The happiness bubbled out of him and he felt that strong desire once more. He wanted the door to be open. He wanted his music to reach the other side. He wanted God to hear what he created. He wanted this as badly as he ever wanted to play music at anytime during his previous life and more. In that same moment, the music simply stopped.

In the dead of silence, Cham came around to the front of the drum set as he looked Steven in the eye.

"What happened?"

At first, Steven said nothing. He looked down at the drumsticks in his hands and then made them and the entire drum set before him disappear.

"What's wrong?" Cham demanded.

"Nothing, it was great, but I had to stop."

"Why?"

"Because it was only me."

"What? You want to play in a band, with others?" Cham asked. "Well, don't let anything stop you. Go ahead. All you have to do is imagine it, let it flow out of you. You want to have Frank or Bing sing along with you? How about the lead guitarist from the latest rock super group? You can do all of that if you want. You just have to imagine it."

"No, that's not it. There was no one else here to listen."

"I'm here. And that's not all. You can create an entire audience if you want. You can play before a small gathering in a club or a giant screaming crowd in some stadium. All of that is possible."

"I know," Steven admitted. "I think I understand that now. If I can imagine it, it can happen here. I get it. It goes beyond just making music. It's anything I can dream about. But that's not what I'm after." Steven pointed to the door in the distance. "There's one thing that won't happen no matter how much I want it to, no matter how much I try to imagine it. That door is still shut."

Cham showed a flash of concern. "You still have that on your mind?"

"It's worse than that. I wanted to go open it. I almost got up and ran to the door, so I had to stop. I was feeling . . . I was just so happy there for a moment that I didn't think I could control myself."

"I see."

"I didn't want to risk it."

"Better safe than sorry," Cham admitted. "Well, maybe we got ahead of ourselves, jumped too far to start off. Music is obviously very important to you, so maybe we should have eased into that."

"Maybe. It was just so great, I just. . . ." Steven's words trailed off as he looked to the door again.

Cham decided to change the focal point. "If we jumped too far, it's only because you've come such a long way. You've moved so fast, and from what you're telling me, it sounds like you really do understand how things work here. You know your imagination powers this place, and it appears you've learned how to let it flow from your being without so much conscious thought. That means you can pretty much do anything here, so why don't we just let you have some fun."

Steven did his best to regroup as he once more buried the elation he felt and allowed calming indifference and cool patience to rule his emotions once more.

"What kind of fun?" Steven asked.

"I'm going to let that be up to you. I'm going to leave for a while and let you experiment on your own for a bit."

"What should I do?"

Cham pondered that question for only an instant and then placed the ultimate direction of any activity back in Steven's hands. "What did you like to do back on earth? What kind of activities made you happy?"

"I liked to read."

"What kind of books? What were some of your favorites?"

"All kinds of books, really. I guess fantasy and science fiction were at the top of the list."

"Excellent. Then why don't you try that. Let your imagination create a story for you. Live it out, enjoy yourself. Fill this space with magic and swords and great battles. Have an adventure. You know you can do it, don't you?"

"Yes, I do."

"Excellent. I'll still be around if you need me. Just give out a call. Otherwise, have a great time."

With that, Cham turned and made his way to a staircase in the distance that the birds had used to leave that same room. He took them as well and marched up and out of sight.

Steven was left alone and ready to create any adventure he could dream up.

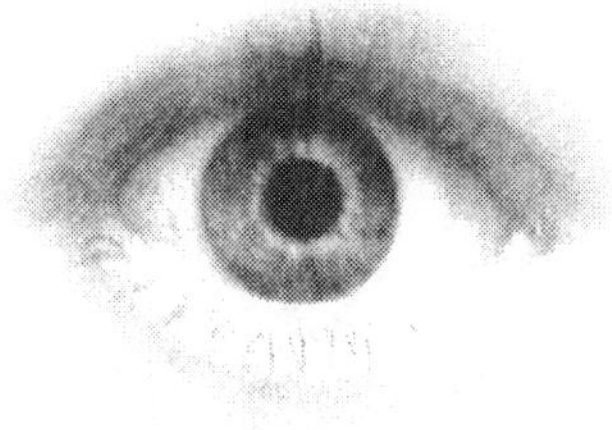

INSIGHT

His new home was not a sprawling castle with spires and towers, grand and imposing at the center of some massive kingdom. Instead, it was a modest house of two stories, brick exterior, and several windows. It did boast a rather large double mahogany door at the center of a wide and comfortable front porch. The structure stood upon open ground, surrounded by well-kept grass in the heart of a meadow with no other homes in sight. Majestic mountains filled the horizon in the far distance to the rear, and the house appeared as the welcoming point for any travelers venturing to see these peaks.

Inside, a friendly atmosphere complemented comfortable furnishings with lots of space to move around. Paintings of peaceful landscapes adorned the walls and the air carried the aroma of freshly baked bread. Almost every room contained a lively burning fireplace, and the dancing flames kept the interior warm and bright.

Very near one of these sturdy, stone-faced fireplaces in a study filled with books, Steven sat at a large desk glancing through the worn, yellowing pages of very old scrolls. He unfurled them carefully and inspected the contents with a curious eye. The writing appeared to be of some strange language that he could not identify but could understand clearly nonetheless. The cryptic symbols formed words he never knew before this moment, and still he knew they carried great power. These were the blueprints of magical incantations.

He read through one spell listing after another, somewhat surprised to find that they were already imprinted in his memory. They were simple instructions, words and actions he already knew, and somehow felt as if he already utilized in both mind and deed. Some summoned great powers of nature for both attack and defense. Others offered illusions and charms to bend the will of others. They all employed powerful magical energies and he knew he could cast them all with ease.

A knock on the door surprised him slightly, he did not expect visitors. Still, he rose from his study without apprehension and moved to the front hall with a casual ease and a curious demeanor. He opened the door boldly, not knowing who or what to expect. Before him was a man that appeared to be of equal age, and somehow Steven understood this visitor was also of equal standing in the power of spell casting.

"Good Day, Steven Icewielder," the guest pronounced.

Steven knew this man to be a friend, though this was the first time he ever truly laid eyes upon him. He also knew that his own last name was no longer Drilach, at least not here and now. In this creation of his imagination, he was known as Icewielder in recognition of his own magical power.

"Good Day to you, Roan of the Dragon," Steven greeted his friend and welcomed him inside without hesitancy or delay. He guided him back into the study.

Before sitting down, Roan asked the question that had brought him here.

"Have you considered my proposal?"

Steven had never spoken to this man before, never heard

this proposal, but it flashed clear in his mind and he stated it back to confirm his understanding.

"You still wish me to freeze certain sections of the Idle Seas in order to create permanent bridges between the Lands of the Trabors and the Islands of Bul?"

"Yes, I think it would be wise," Roan nodded. "The island people of Bul are not well equipped as seafaring people. They can not leave their island, but if they do not open trade routes with Trabor, they can not flourish. The ice bridges will allow them that."

"That may be," Steven replied as he envisioned these islands as if he had visited them countless times before. The entire scene was a dreamlike sequence being played out and Steven stood at the center of the plot. The story, the characters, the surrounding lands all flowed freely from his imagination, and though he had never been in the house before, spoken with this wizard at any other time, or even heard of the people of Bul, he was keenly aware of each and every characteristic as if he had lived a lifetime in this place. "It would also block the path for those that *are* seafaring people. I must always consider the. . . ."

Another knock at the door interrupted Steven's response. This knock, however, continued angrily. The thumping grew to a fierce pounding and soon the very walls began to shake.

Instinctively, Steven waved his hands and muttered words he never spoke before. A shield of ice covered the inner walls of his study just as the structure around them exploded into shards of brick and wood.

The contents of the study, including the two wizards, remained intact, but now they stood under an open sky with nothing to block the view of the surrounding fields. Steven peered through the crystal clear ice wall that protected them from the blast. With nothing remaining of his house outside the ice barrier, he could see right to the front walkway, and stare down the trespassers that clearly wished to cause him harm.

One in particular stood in front of all the others, staring

hungrily back into the ice dome. Steven recognized this creature, and while Roan was his ally, this invader was without doubt an enemy.

"You destroyed my home, Gaisaon," Steven leveled at the lean, athletic figure that did not even bother to hide in the shadows. "And you lack the courage to face me alone."

The tall sleek body of the cat-like creature stood at the front of well over four dozen other such monsters. Gaisaon hissed back at the wizards behind the ice, then reared his head back and screeched in a caterwaul to emphasize his own fury.

As with Roan, Steven had never seen this Gaisaon creature before—had never read about him in some past novel or heard about him from some old fable. Yet still, he knew his enemy's name and his powers, knew that he was a powerful foe, but one that he did not fear.

"You were always one to make noise," Steven said. "Your wails, however, have always fallen on deaf ears here."

"You will truly be deaf when I slice your ears from your head," the monster screeched, "and blind when I claw out your eyes, and speechless when I tear the tongue from your pathetic mouth."

"He has many allies with him this time," Roan cautioned in a whisper, "perhaps too many even for the two of us."

Steven understood this caution all too well. The ice shield would not hold indefinitely against such strength of numbers. If allowed to reach the crystal wall, the cat creatures would shatter it in moments. Still, he understood his own powers even though he had never unleashed them until this very moment.

"They are many and they are quick, this is true," Steven replied, "but they are also earthbound and a slippery ground shall even the odds."

With a wave of his hands and a shout of magical power, sheets of ice flowed from Steven covering the ground in every direction. Even the ground below the feet of his adversaries froze to a perfectly smooth surface. Steven then called a quick command to his single ally.

"Hit them with your fury, but not your fire! Leave the ice intact."

Roan understood and did not unleash the dragon breath that was his to command. Dragons, however, also have wings and a tail that can unleash powerful forces of their own. When replicated by magical energies, hurricane winds and the blunt destructive power of a potent scaled club can batter even the mightiest fortress.

Whispering incantations of his own, Roan projected these forces of a dragon at the cat monsters that now stood unsteadily upon frozen ground. The fury of the spell shattered Steven's ice dome but it also sent their enemies sprawling into rocks and tall weeds that waited at the ends of the ice sheets.

"Well done," Steven said with a grin. He felt more than simple camaraderie with this wizard, he sensed fellowship and respect. He knew he could depend on Roan, that he and his friend shared a brotherhood in the magic they commanded. He was grateful for the wizard's presence at this moment, a refreshing realization that he was not alone to face this challenge.

With renewed confidence, Steven turned his attention back to his foes. Although he knew Gaisaon to be a despicable creature of treachery, Steven still gave the monster a chance for salvation. "Leave now Gaisaon and renounce your evil while there's still time. Even with a hundred more allies, you could not hope to defeat me alone, but as you can see I am not alone. I can freeze your bones in an instant or my friend can burn you to ash. Don't press for either fate, because if you persist, on this day you will most certainly meet one or the other."

Gaisaon hissed once more and then shouted commands to his own allies. The creatures used their feline abilities to deftly respond. They jumped back to their feet and circled about in no clear formation. Their own speed was impressive as they became mere blurs of motion. Their claws cut into the ice sheets which gave them some level of mobility on the slick surface.

Realizing that this was not a call to retreat, Steven shook his head sadly. "So be it." He then turned to Roan. "Hold your power in reserve. It will probably not be necessary, but caution is almost always rewarded. For now, leave them to me."

Roan bowed slightly in acceptance of the request.

Looking first to the skies above him, Steven drank in the magical energies that resided here as naturally as the air. His form pulsated with power as he clasped his hands in front of him in prayer-like form. He focused all of his inner force on the creation of a circle to surround him and his friend, and a blazing ring of cold blue magic formed entirely about them. Steven uttered words of a foreign tongue and punctuated them with a shout of pure will.

The blue ring began to swirl as it turned and spun in a clockwise rotation. The raging power remained contained in this circle of pure energy as Steven would not allow it to strike out haphazardly. It would only strike those that meant them harm.

"Leave now! This is your last warning," Steven cried out.

Three of the feline creatures pounced toward Steven simultaneously albeit from different directions. They moved with such swiftness that even Roan blessed with the natural speed of a dragon did not spot all three.

The surrounding magic, however, moved at a far greater speed. Blue lightning shot out from the ring, striking all three forms at the peak of their leaps. Each creature turned to stone-like ice and then fell like anvils to the ground with resounding thuds.

The display gave pause to a few of the attacking creatures, but not all. Several moved in from behind, hoping to reach Steven unaware.

Steven, however, could now perceive everything about him. He was aware of the creatures before they decided to spring, and once more cold lightning flashed in a crackle of dark blue streaks.

As his enemies fell around him, Steven felt the exuberance of wielding great power against malevolent foes. At this moment, he knew he was the hero, the mighty sorcerer that utilized magic to defeat evil. He was the champion that honored all that was just and right. He was not fighting for the sake of violence, he was not attacking out of the desire to be vicious. These villains intended to strike at him, and he merely defended himself with absolute justification.

As more of the monsters fell to Steven's awesome spell, the remainder finally understood the futility of their endeavor and raced well out of sight. Only Gaisaon remained, and he crouched low in a defensive posture, all the time looking for some weakness to exploit.

With full control of the magic at his disposal, Steven uttered a few words and the ring of winter power dissolved at his command. He waved his hand in front of him and the ice sheets on the ground melted away to a mist that evaporated quickly in the air. He took a few steps forward on dry ground to ensure that Roan was several paces behind him. He now wished to face Gaisaon on his own.

"Your allies are gone and my friend has been instructed to remain silent in this," Steven spoke with an edge of certainty. "You have failed once more and this time others have paid the price for your hateful actions. You commanded these puppets and they attacked at your bequest. Have you no remorse?"

"Remorse?" Gaisaon screeched. "I think not. The world is filled with minions and they are here to do the bidding of their masters, even if it means their destruction. What do I care for them? I can always find more."

"I'm afraid that is no longer true. I gave you the chance to leave peacefully. You wasted that chance and others died for your foolishness. I won't allow others to suffer in the future.

You've made your choice, it is now time you dealt with the consequences of your actions."

Gaisaon did not wait for further explanation. Believing he finally had his chance, he leapt with all his might upon his enemy wizard with claws extended ready to rip out Steven's heart.

Steven, however, was not caught unsuspecting. The spell was already on his lips as he clapped his hands before him. The full power of a north winter wind exploded from his palms and bore into Gaisaon with indescribable fury. The monster disintegrated in midair.

Steven said nothing—no shout of victory and no display of arrogant superiority. He looked upon Gaisaon's hollow attempt with disgust as well as dismay. Such a creature should never be allowed to exist.

Roan stepped up beside his friend and placed a hand on his shoulder. "You did what needed to be done."

"Such a waste," Steven responded solemnly.

"Perhaps," Roan continued, "but the consequences were his to choose as is always the case. We can only stand before God's final judgment and know that in His mercy He will understand what is truly in our hearts."

These words caught Steven's total attention. There was something more to them, some deep meaning that went well beyond a casual remark in some fantasy story. He expected comfort from his friend, but the mention of God carried more weight than he would have guessed, and in that, he looked for clarification.

"Why do you say that?"

Roan spoke sincerely, looking Steven straight in the eye. "We all face the burden of paying for our mistakes and our misjudgments in some way. Sometimes, however, our mistakes don't match our intentions. You destroyed Gaisaon, that is indisputable, but it was not your action that began this sequence of events, nor was it truly your intention to destroy him. Gaisaon came here of his own choice, refused a chance to leave in peace.

He left you with little choice and so you acted. He is gone now by your hand. In my estimation, your actions were honorable and if God must judge you, it will be based on the full scope of the circumstances and not on the final conclusion."

"You think I am to be judged by this?"

"We are judged by many things. We also tend to judge ourselves. I hear in your words and see in your heart that you possibly feel regret. That is understandable, but now let me take this one step further, do you think you should be punished for what you have done?"

Steven marveled at this question. Roan was a creation of Steven's mind, his own imagination, of that he was certain, and yet Roan now asked a complex philosophical question that Steven could not completely answer.

"I'm not sure," Steven replied as he reflected on the events that just occurred. "If I'm to be honest about this, I have to consider what really happened. Maybe I should have acted differently. I'm not sure exactly what led to this, but I may not be completely blameless in the matter. Gaisaon came here for me, that means his quarrel was with me. Maybe I could have found a way to avoid this conflict altogether."

"And maybe it would have happened regardless of what you did. Perhaps it was your destiny to face this situation. Many times a person is put in circumstances he or she did not ask for. People don't always get what they deserve, and certainly there are times they get things they don't deserve. Certainly you understand that."

"If you're saying things are not always fair, I agree, but that doesn't mean I shouldn't have tried to avoid conflict."

"But you did try, and still conflict occurred. That's not your fault. Often things just happen because they can not be avoided, regardless of whether they are earned or not."

"If that's the case, then what choice did I really have?" Steven asked aloud, but the question was really for his own contemplation. "If I couldn't avoid the situation, then how else could I have handled it?"

"That might be the true question before you," Roan offered.

"Well, there's the thought I should have done nothing. I didn't have to cast that last spell."

Roan rejected that idea. "It is clear to me Gaisaon would not have been satisfied until one of you were dead."

"Maybe I should have just let him win."

"And if he succeeded in killing you, what then? He would have also attacked me. Should I have let him succeed in that? If I fought back and won, Gaisaon would still be dead. If I lost, then I would be dead. And what would your part be in my death? If you sacrificed your own life to avoid confronting Gaisaon, that would be one thing, but it may have also meant sacrificing my life. And if so, would my destruction be on your conscience then just as Gaisaon's is on it now?"

Steven knew the entire episode did not actually occur. It was nothing more than a dream played out for no one but himself. There was no Gaisaon and there was no Roan. It shouldn't matter if either one had been killed in this scene, as they were nothing more than imaginary creations. For some reason, however, Roan's point seemed to hold something more important.

"You're saying that I would have been guilty in some way no matter what I did?" Steven pressed.

"Do you feel guilty?"

This was truly the question Steven did not know how to face. Despite the few moments of exhilaration within this fantasy, he had buried his feelings, kept them in control under the guise of patience.

"I'm not sure I feel anything. I haven't been sure about that since I got here."

"You are stifling your feelings then?" Roan pressed.

"Yes, I am."

"Why?"

"Because I'm worried they might lead me to a mistake."

Roan gave that concern its due credit, but only to a point. "Emotions can do that, but only when they are selfish emotions. When you focus only on what you want and to fulfill your own desires, then certainly they can lead you astray. Not all desires, however, will put us on the wrong path. There is the desire to do what is right, the desire to live by honor. When fighting Gaisaon, you had the desire to be merciful. You gave him the chance to leave. You also had the desire to protect me. That is why you shielded me. These were honorable intentions, and burying these desires would be a very bad thing."

"So then by stifling all my emotions, I'm suppressing the good along with the bad?"

"Another question for you to ponder," Roan responded with a nod.

"I don't have to ponder that one, I know the answer," Steven admitted. There was a greater truth here, an understanding beyond the ultimate demise of Gaisaon. Steven was forcing himself to face the consequences of his decision to suppress his emotions. It might have kept his desires in check, but at what cost? "If I become ambivalent to everything, then I have no moral compass. At that point, nothing matters at all. If I stop caring, then I crush the desire to do the right thing along with those desires that might lead me to a mistake."

Roan smiled broadly. "And if you trust yourself to do what is right, then how bad can the mistake be?"

And here, Steven's cautious nature returned to the forefront of his thoughts. The debate was no longer centered on whether killing Gaisaon was defensible, but on whether Steven should smother his desire to see God. If he allowed that desire to rule, he would have to consider the warnings he received from Cham.

"That's the problem, this could be a mistake that might have dire consequences."

"For you, or someone else?" Roan asked.

"Just me, as far as I can tell."

"Then maybe it's a mistake worth making."

"What if the mistake takes me away from God?"

"Are you with God now?"

"No," Steven said sadly.

"Then it seems to me you have little to lose. Rather than being afraid of doing what's wrong, you might want to consider doing what is right. There can be a difference. Consider what is it you wish to do. Is this action based solely on a selfish desire?"

"I don't think so, but I don't know."

"I think you do, deep down you must."

"Deep down I don't think it's a mistake. I think it's something I need to do and I really don't think I'm defying God. It's just that I'm confused. I don't know enough of what's going on here."

"And don't you think God knows this?" Roan asked. "I'm not saying you can justify a treacherous act with some noble goal. God can not be so easily deceived. He will always know the truth. That being said, if it is not your intention to defy God, then why would He possibly see it otherwise?"

Steven could not believe what he was hearing. A character out of his imagination was actually justifying what he wanted to do with all his soul. He was hearing a clear and sound argument to remove the doubts and confusion from his mind and to throw open the door that blocked him from God.

He wanted to simply take that advice and move toward that end with no regrets, yet as always, he remained cautious and he felt the need to tie this advice to the scene that brought Roan to him in the first place.

"What does all this have to do with what happened here with Gaisaon?"

Roan responded as if Steven should have already known the answer. "Intentions, actions, and consequences—three aspects blurred into one dilemma—that is the common denominator."

It was as simple as that and Steven needed no further explanation.

"Thank you, Roan."

Steven said no more to this wizard that came from the depths of his soul. He simply wiped the entire scene—Roan included—from his sight. The space before him returned to the empty, white room that met him on his entry into the afterlife. He saw the door against the far wall. It remained closed. He took one step toward it before hearing one last heed for caution.

"You really don't want to do that," Cham's voice called out.

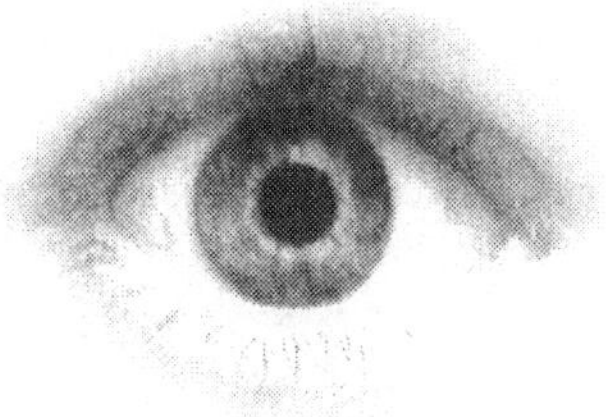

HESITATION

So you're going to just forget everything we talked about and go open that door?" Cham asked.

Steven turned about. He had no idea where Cham came from, but that caused him little surprise. Steven just spent time in a fantasy world born out of his imagination. He created Roan and Gaisaon and he lived through a battle of monsters and magic. And moments ago, he made it all disappear with a simple thought. There really was no reason for him to be shocked or even mildly surprised by Cham's sudden appearance out of no where.

"I haven't forgotten anything," Steven responded.

"Well you must have forgotten something, because it's pretty clear to me what you're about to do."

"I don't deny it. It's time to open that door."

Cham's expression revealed his annoyance and he circled halfway around Steven, planting himself directly between Steven and the door in the distance.

"So says you."

"That's right. Are you going to stop me?" Steven asked defiantly.

"I can't stop you. You can shove right through me and there's not a damn thing I can do about that, but that doesn't mean I'm going to give up. I can still try to save you from yourself."

Steven felt a growing animosity building toward Cham. For some reason, he sensed Cham was now less a guide and more of an obstacle, something placed in his way.

"Look, I don't mean to be rude, but why don't you just step aside and let me do what I have to do."

"I could do that, but then again, is that what you really want? I think you should consider why I'm here."

"You told me why you're here. You're here to answer some questions and show me what I can do in this place. Well, you've done that, but now I'm facing a larger issue, one that's between me and God, and you have nothing to do with it."

"Are you so sure?"

A twinge of uncertainty suddenly bit at Steven. "What do you mean? Are you saying you do have something to do with whether or not I see God?"

Cham sounded almost belligerent. "If so, it's only because you allowed it. And you best not simply disregard what I just said, because it's important. The one thing you can be totally sure of here is that you control this space, you know that to be true, don't you?"

"Yes, I understand that, but. . . ."

"No, just stop. Don't try to make excuses, and don't try to twist things around. It's a simple concept. You control this space. That means you allowed me in here. I could not have shown up unless you allowed it. Deep down, you know that's true."

It was true. Steven could not deny it. He filled this space; he controlled it with the spirit of his imagination. Cham was here because Steven let him in.

Cham seized on this new understanding. "That's right. I'm here because part of you wants me here. And in that alone, you have to give me at least some consideration. For you to really understand what's going on here, you can't simply ignore me. You may not want to agree with me, but it would be sheer recklessness to disregard me completely." Cham punctuated this with a question that could not be easily answered. "If you control this space and I meant nothing to you, then why am I here?"

The uncertainty grew.

"I'm not sure why you're really here," Steven replied, "but I don't think you're here to help me, maybe at first, but not anymore."

"Maybe I am and maybe I'm not. The problem is you just admitted you're not sure why I'm here. If you're not sure about that, how can you be sure of anything? Specifically, how can you be sure that opening that door is the right thing to do?"

Steven looked to the door. He felt the warmth radiating from it. It did more than welcome him, it called to him, and a new determination fought back against the uncertainty. "Because I'm looking at things differently now. I can't simply sit back and let a closed door stop me, and that's really all it is. It's just a closed door and I need to see it as that and nothing more."

Cham raised an eyebrow. "And that's all there is to it? You just decide to come up with a new viewpoint and you think that's going to justify doing something you shouldn't do?"

"First of all, I'm not so sure I shouldn't do it," Steven said with a resoluteness growing within him. "It's a door that leads to God. You told me that and I know it's true, I can feel it . . . I'm certain about that."

"Well good. I'm glad we agree on that. And since you realize that, you should also know it's not just an ordinary closed door. It's not something you just throw open. There's more to it than that."

"Of course there's more to it than that, but I don't see any reason not to open it. I don't sense any imminent danger. If anything, I'm pulled toward that door. Only when I bury my feelings do I think it's a good idea to stay here and wait for it to open on its own. You're the one that told me to do that, and I don't think that's the best advice. I'm starting to realize that I have to trust my own judgment."

"Well that makes perfect sense, and of course, you shouldn't listen to me," Cham responded with more than a hint of sarcasm. "It's better to just disregard everything I say, or in this case, do the exact opposite. If I might ask, what could possibly have given you this idea in the first place, to trust your own judgment over my advice? Where did this piece of wisdom come from?"

Steven paused. At first, he did not want to argue the point. Did he *want* to tell Cham about his discussion with Roan? Did he *need* to? The answer to both was no, and yet he felt he owed Cham an explanation. So, he gave him one.

"I started thinking about it when you left me here to make my own adventure. You told me to experiment with this place, so I did. I created a fantasy story with magic and wizards. It might sound silly, but it doesn't matter. One of the wizards pointed out that there's more to any action than just the results. There are intentions involved as well, and that got me thinking."

Cham actually laughed out loud. "You've got to be kidding me. You're going to take some imaginary figure seriously when it comes to something as important as this? This is God we're talking about. You're not sneaking a look behind some curtain and you're not opening a Christmas present early. This is about the biggest decision you could possibly make. Don't you think that it's incredibly foolish to listen to some character that popped out of your imagination?"

At this, Steven felt compelled to defend himself and once more he viewed Cham not as an ally but as the opposition. "It's not foolish! Maybe it seems that way to you, but you're not looking at it the same way I am. I'm taking it seriously, and do you know why? Because this wizard was not just an imaginary figure, not completely. He came from inside of me. Yes, my imagination created him, but his words had to come from somewhere and they came from me. They came from deep down, something I was feeling. I may have put a lid on those feelings, but they wouldn't stay buried completely. They fought to get out. That has to mean something. I can't just dismiss it."

"And maybe you shouldn't dismiss it," Cham countered. "Maybe you just need to take a good look at what you're saying. You just referred to intentions being important. So what are your intentions now? You're just going to ignore my advice and throw open that door even though I'm telling you it's not time. If intentions are important, then don't you think it's your intention to barge in on God? And maybe you have other intentions as well, who knows what you're thinking at this point. You could be flat out defying God without hesitation."

"Absolutely not! That's not my intention at all. I certainly don't want to defy God, and I believe He'll know that."

"You *believe*, but you're not sure. So you are basing this all on a guess, some vague perception that you can understand God's will?"

"No," Steven stated. "It's not some vague perception. It's more than that. It's what I'm feeling when I'm not burying my emotions."

"Trusting emotions is a dangerous thing."

"I know that, but ignoring them entirely can be just as dangerous. When you remove all emotion, you stop caring, and that includes caring about what's right and wrong. If I just accept apathy, then nothing matters. What do I care if God wants to see me or not? What do I care if I wait here for an eternity? You see? When you bury things, nothing matters, not even the important stuff—but if I allow myself to care, then I have to actually face certain decisions. I can try to understand my emotions as well as where they might lead me. If my intentions are honorable, then my emotions should do me justice. They can give me direction as long as I'm honest with myself."

"Yes, honesty is important," Cham allowed. "With that

in mind, didn't your wizard friend also say something about consequences?"

Steven never spoke of consequences to Cham.

"How did you know that?" Steven demanded, now eyeing Cham with even more suspicion.

"I'm a part of this place, too," Cham answered. "Even though I was not a participant in your fantasy story, your consciousness echoes throughout this space. There are imprints of your thoughts that can be perceived like waves of old memories. I don't rely only on what I *see* or what I *hear*. My perceptions go much deeper than that, and maybe that's why you shouldn't disregard my advice. I know what this wizard of your dream told you."

Steven did not back down. If anything, he felt greater confidence. "That's good. Then you should know what I'm talking about. It's not all about the actions we take, it's why we take them, and yes, there are consequences for those actions, both bad and good. The three are intertwined—intentions, actions, and consequences."

"And are you prepared for the consequences should you be wrong?"

"I'm prepared to let God judge me on what's in my heart."

"That's not what I asked. I asked if you're ready for the consequences. What happens if God doesn't want you to open that door and you defy Him anyway? Do you even know what the consequences are? Maybe it's time I showed you."

Steven did not anticipate this, and though he felt no true fear, an unsettling doubt over his expectations began to form.

"How can you show me the consequences for doing something that's not wrong?"

"Well, that's what you say, but what if you *are* wrong? You think you're right. You want to believe in your instincts or emotions or feelings . . . or whatever it is that's driving you down this path to oblivion, but can you be absolutely certain? If there's even the slightest chance you might have made a miscalculation, don't you owe it to yourself to see what could happen?"

"I don't know. . . ."

"I think you should know. You said it yourself, the words of the wizard came from inside you and he didn't just speak of intentions and actions. He mentioned consequences. There has to be a reason that was included. Wouldn't you agree?"

Steven said nothing.

"Only a fool takes such a risk without understanding all the possible outcomes, especially the most serious consequences. Come with me," Cham ordered, and he turned toward the set of stairs that previously led them back to the remains of Steven's house back on earth.

"You're taking me back to earth?"

"Yes."

"Why are we going back there?"

"Why? You're asking me why?" Cham stopped, turned back to Steven, and tilted his head in a show of surprise. "So you can get just a taste of hell. You'd be surprised how miserable things can be there, but I can show you."

Steven resisted. He felt as if his argument had been turned against him in an illogical fashion. He believed it was his intentions that were important, not the consequences. Still, he could not argue that consequences had been part of his discussion with Roan. It just seemed as if they were suddenly focusing on the wrong area.

"You don't want to see?" Cham persisted. "Are you going to be selective about how you view things? That seems to be a decision of convenience as opposed to an intention to find the truth. If you still want to go open that door, I think you should hear me out—unless of course you've changed your mind and want to leave the door closed until it's the proper time."

"No, I haven't changed my mind. I just don't think it's necessary to go back to earth. I remember what happened the last time I went back there."

"I guess you're talking about that overwhelming sorrow that nearly crushed you out of existence, is that right?"

"Yeah, that's part of it."

"Well, that's not what I want you to experience. I'm not trying to cause you pain, I'm just trying to expand your knowledge. That's what this place is all about."

"You said I could go through that pain again if I stayed too long back there, remember?"

"Of course I remember, but you've grown a bit. Not enough so that you're ready to open that door, mind you, but enough that you should be steady enough to avoid another emotional attack back on earth."

"Then what's the point of going back?"

"Like I said, I want to show you something that's going to expand your knowledge. When you first came here, you asked me about hell. I didn't want to talk about it because I thought you were smart enough to avoid it. I guess I thought wrong."

"So what, you're going to take me to hell now?"

"No, I'm not capable of doing that, but I can at least give you a taste of what it's like, and believe me, once you get the smallest taste, you'll think twice about taking any chances."

"And what if I don't go with you now?"

"That's your choice. I can't force you to do anything you don't want to do. If you want to go throw open that door, go ahead, but that's not what we're talking about anymore is it?"

"I'm not sure what we're talking about."

"Yes, you do. You said your wizard friend gave you some advice. You want to listen to it, but apparently not all of it."

"Again, it wasn't just some imaginary wizard that said this, it came from me. That's why I think it's so important."

"Fine, you want to listen to your own advice. You believe you want to trust your feelings. You think you should allow your emotions to be heard because they give you a sense of caring about what's right and what's wrong, but what about those consequences we talked about, hmmmm?"

"I haven't forgotten," Steven stated.

"Maybe you haven't forgotten about them, but it seems you may be ignoring them. If all this insight you keep referring to came from inside of you, then you have to consider the whole thing—intentions, actions, and *consequences*. Wouldn't it be foolish to act without understanding the consequences?"

"I'm not afraid of the consequences because I understand my intentions," Steven persisted.

"I don't think you do understand your intentions, but we'll get to that. Even if you're right about all of this, then why not just humor me and take a look at what I have to show you? What do you have to lose? Time? There are no clocks here."

For the first time since he appeared in the afterlife, Steven actually experienced complete confusion. This was not like the moment when he faced accepting his own death. That was a simple decision with two clear paths. Either he accepted the fact that he died, or he did not. Here, he was not so sure of all his options. He knew he could follow Cham. He also knew he could ignore Cham and simply move to the door. Unfortunately, they were not mutually exclusive. He could go with Cham and still return to open the door to God. He could also refuse both, at least temporarily. Instead of opening the door or returning to earth with Cham, he could go back to some other dreamlike fantasy. He could even bring Roan back and continue the debate with him, which in essence would be like talking to himself.

Steven looked upon the door and made a quick decision. He vowed he would open it, but he had to acknowledge two factors. First, consequences were part of this decision and knowing those consequences should not be a deterrent to doing what's right. Second, he knew deep down that he allowed Cham to come before him. For some reason, he believed he had to hear Cham through to the end.

Cham was also right about there not being any clocks in this place. Steven had the time to gather as much knowledge as possible. It wasn't like he had an appointment time with God.

Ultimately, Steven realized one more important factor that assisted him in his decision. He knew he could return to this place at his own wish. He understood that without doubt. Even if he went back to earth with Cham, Cham could not stop Steven from coming back here.

"Fine," Steven finally responded. "I'll go see what it is you want to show me, but don't be disappointed when I don't change my mind about what I have to do."

"Tell me that again when I'm done," Cham said as he turned back to the stairs that led to earth.

Steven followed quietly.

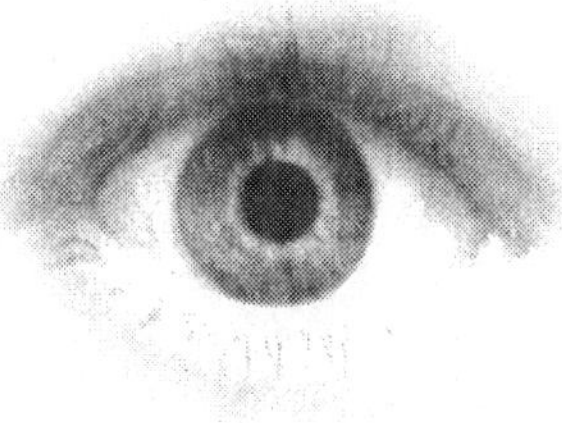

CONFUSION

"Consequences only matter when you are afraid of them, when you don't believe what you're doing is right," Steven said to himself as he steeled his nerves against the unimaginable. As he descended the steps bracing for unknown terrors, he knew Cham wanted to convince him to stay away from the door to God. The only way that was going to be possible was to reveal horrors that would haunt him for all eternity. Cham had stated he wanted to reveal a glimpse of hell, and Steven expected no less.

"What was that?" Cham asked, although he heard Steven's words clear enough.

"Nothing, just reminding myself of what's important."

"You do that."

And so Steven vowed he would. He decided to face this moment as a way to fortify his conviction. He would prove not only to Cham, but also to himself, that he fully understood the implications of his decisions, and that his actions would be based on his honorable intentions. He would not fall to fear.

With one final step from the stairs, the white walls and

stone staircase melted away. Steven and Cham stood once more on earth amid green trees during another bright sunny day.

Steven looked about and realized he was back at the banks of the river that flowed near his home, the river that had flooded and caused his death. He stood downstream from his old yard, but he still recognized the area.

He wondered what could possibly be so terrible in this place that it would make him change his mind about wanting to see God. Other than the rush of the waters next to him and the chirping of birds in the trees, he heard nothing that would indicate some horrible vision of unending anguish.

"This is supposed to give me an idea of what hell is like?" Steven asked as he found nothing about him that would indicate such terror. There were no shrieks of pain, and no screams of torment. Just the peaceful ordinary sounds of a calm, summer day.

Steven took a quick glance at Cham and realized his guide was staring into the middle of the river. Steven followed that gaze to the gray mist he remembered from his last journey to this place.

The lost soul of the woman had not left her spot in the river. The gray fog that marked her being remained half in the slow running waters and half exposed to the warm summer air.

Once again, Steven felt great sadness for this poor spirit, but he could not guess as to the purpose of this return visit.

"Why did you bring me back here?" Steven asked.

"Because I wanted you to see what agony and suffering are like," Cham offered. "We are here because it's time for you to fully understand everything that you face. You want to talk about intentions, actions, and consequences. This woman's situation encompasses all three."

"I thought you only wanted to deal with the consequences," Steven questioned.

"That would be letting you off easy, and I have no intention of doing that. We're going to deal with everything your wizard friend discussed and here is the perfect example."

"The perfect example of what? You told me she couldn't accept her own death. What's that got to do with me?"

"It has quite a bit to do with you. She's going to help me show you what real emptiness feels like."

"And why do I have to feel that?"

"Because that's what you're risking. If you make the wrong decision, you'll be facing emptiness you can't imagine. You really don't understand as much as you'd like to believe. Your experiences are still mired in your mortal existence, so we need to change that. But before we do, let's talk about that old life of yours for a moment. You were always cautious about things back then, am I right?"

"Yes."

"You were sensible and you saw the foolishness in the rash actions of others. For those that took silly risks with their lives, you thought they stupidly played with death. Isn't this also true?"

Steven was at a total loss to understand the point of this. "Yes, it's true, so what?"

"I'm here to help you put your situation in context, to examine your previous life in terms of what you're thinking of doing now. If you really are in such a hurry to see God, then you best take some time to seriously consider your true feelings. The first thing I'm asking you is why you would want to take such a monumental risk in the first place. If in life you regarded taking enormous risks as a foolhardy endeavor, then why would you be willing to take such a risk now?"

Steven answered with confidence, allowing his response to come not from some logical argument, but from the feelings deep in his soul. "Because I think it's the right thing to do."

"Even if the risk is beyond anything you can measure? In your old life, I would dare say you would think that the height of stupidity."

"What I'm contemplating has nothing to do with my old life."

"Then again, maybe it does. Your life on earth shaped your character. You've said you want to let your feelings guide you.

Wouldn't it then be smart to understand those feelings? If you wish to talk about intentions, actions, and consequences, then we need to put them in a framework that corresponds to your personal circumstances."

"Okay, fine. I do want to trust my feelings, and I admit I've always been cautious. But one doesn't necessarily cancel out the other. You can trust your instincts, believe in your feelings, and still not take risks that you know are just plain stupid."

"How can you say that if you don't fully comprehend the scope of what you want to do?" Cham questioned. "The risk you are putting yourself at now is far worse than any foolish action you could ever imagine. If you were alive once more and dangling on a thin thread over a pool of lava, that would be child's play compared to what you want to do now. I want you to understand that."

"How? By showing me this woman again? I'm not risking what she's going through."

Cham shifted his gaze from the center of the river to the center of Steven's being.

"It bothers you to see her again, doesn't it? I haven't even shown you what I want to show you, and you're already very upset. Why is that?"

Steven remained quiet. He was not going to explain himself. It was not his intention to help Cham in any way.

Cham, however, pounced. "You want to help her, but it goes deeper than that. You don't understand how she can be allowed to suffer. That's what really bothers you, isn't it?"

"I don't like to see anybody suffer," Steven admitted.

"And yet you wish to expose yourself to suffering you can't imagine. I brought you here so I could let you experience what it is she's going through. I can show you how it feels to be in her situation."

Steven felt no fear of facing any torment, but he could not understand the purpose.

"What's that going to prove? She never accepted death. I

understand that, but that's not what we're talking about. I've accepted my death. The disagreement we're having is whether or not I should seek God now that I am dead."

"That's the way you want to put it," Cham argued. "That's not how I see it. I keep telling you that you're trying to force your wishes on God. When you do that, you're just asking for more trouble than you can fathom. You're asking to be cast out, to be lost, just like her."

"What am I missing here?" Steven pressed back. "I've already seen this woman. This isn't going to change my mind."

"Don't be so sure. You've only seen the surface. You have no idea how deep her torment goes. I can't take you to hell, but I can show you a spirit completely separated from God."

"But that's what I'm saying," Steven protested. "I don't want to be separated from God, either. That's why I want to open the door."

"NO!" Cham shouted and the strain in his tone shocked Steven. "You've always separated yourself from God! Throughout your life you separated yourself from God. It's time you understand that. It's time you face some truths."

"What truths?" Steven demanded.

"The truth that you are not content with God's will and you want to force your own will on the situation."

"Why do you keep making this some kind of battle of wills?"

"Because that is what you have made it! You made it that from the very beginning. Think back, back to when you used to have a mortal existence. What did you think of God?"

"I believed in Him," Steven responded with a firm demeanor of confidence.

"Of course you did, but what did you think of Him?"

"What did I think of Him? What kind of question is that? God is God. I just accepted He existed and that I would get the answers when I finally saw Him."

"What answers?" Cham demanded.

"The answers to life's questions."

"Ah, and so we get to the true point. The questions of life, that's what you call them now, but what you mean is you had your doubts. You looked at the world and you couldn't understand it. You wondered how there could be so much pain and suffering in this world. Isn't that one of your questions?"

Steven did not respond. This is not what he wanted to discuss, not what he agreed to return to earth to witness.

Cham pressured Steven for an answer. "I can tell by looking at you that this bothers you. You may not have questioned God's existence, but you always, always questioned his intentions. Didn't you?"

"I don't know . . . maybe."

"There's no *maybe* about it. Let's not dance about the truth. You saw things you didn't like, things that were so obviously wrong."

"Of course I did, everyone does."

Then a gleam grew in Cham's eyes as he stared back into the river. "That's what's really bothering you about this lost soul. You think it's wrong for her to have to go through this. I haven't even told you her story yet, and you can't believe she's out here suffering. You can't believe God allows that, can you?"

"I don't know what to believe about that. Like you said, I don't know her story."

"But you still don't like it, do you?"

Steven felt a hollowness open deeper in his soul, a bad memory forced to resurface, and he didn't appreciate it one bit.

"Of course not, it would be wrong to enjoy seeing anyone tormented."

"Wrong based on what?" Cham challenged. "Based on your judgment? That's the true point of all this, isn't it? You think you know more than God, you always thought you knew better than God. You always believed that God shouldn't allow certain things, but He did anyway. He allowed this world to be filled with injustice and you could never resolve that, could you?"

"No, I couldn't!" Steven shot back. "I didn't understand it. I still don't." It was out in the open now, an admission made.

Cham seized the opportunity.

"And now you want to know why. You want to throw open that door and question God's motives. Don't you? Isn't that your true intention?"

"No!"

"No?"

Steven finally explained his intentions as he understood them.

"I'm tired of questioning things I can't understand. I don't have the answers. How can I question the motives of things I can't understand? The world wasn't created just so it could make sense to me. I figured that out a while ago."

"But it still bothers you, even to this moment, even after you've died. There's a question that burns in your mind. *Why?* Why does God let people suffer? That's what you want to know." It went deeper than that, and somehow Cham knew and he would not relent. "You used to blame God for the suffering. You cursed Him for being so negligent, for not appearing to care. That's what you're really afraid to face. You think you want to see God right now, but even you know you might not be ready. You found fault with God, and that scares you. In fact, almost everything about this world bothers you. You see all the pain and you can't figure out why it exists, can you?"

Steven would not answer. It was no longer an old memory thrown in his face. Now it was a deep wound that Cham had ripped the scab off and stabbed repeatedly.

Cham showed no sympathy and continued to demand answers. "Maybe the real question I should ask you is not why you're in such a hurry to open the door, but why was it closed in the first place? You don't like what you've seen of this world, just like you don't like what happened to that poor soul out in the river. Isn't that right?"

"I'm not ashamed to say that!" Steven finally fired back. "Of course I don't like it, only a sadistic bastard would. And maybe

I did blame God, but that was a long time ago. I don't blame Him anymore. I stopped long before I died. That's what you just don't get. Yes, my emotions get the better of me sometimes, but that's better than just burying them. I used to get upset and I used to get mad when I saw things that didn't make sense. And yes, there was a time I would blame God, but that's not driving me anymore. I don't want to see God because I want to question Him about all the pain and suffering. I'm tired of being separated from Him. There's nothing left to keep me away but that stupid door. Opening it is not about me defying Him. It's about me giving in, and that's what I plan on doing."

Cham remained quiet for long moments, as if he was not prepared for that statement. Finally, he pointed out to the gray mist in the middle of the river.

"You want to know why this woman is here? I'll tell you. More years ago than you can imagine, she and her family were riding a riverboat down this river. While she was at the front of the boat watching the scenery, her ten-year-old boy came up behind her and pushed her over the railing. Her son pushed her, do you follow me?"

Cham paused to let that point sink in.

"Yes, I got it," Steven said sadly.

"I can see it if it happened yesterday," Cham continued as he gazed off into the waters. "The boy wasn't large. He was an average-sized ten-year-old, but his mother was a smallish woman and she didn't expect the shove. He jabbed her right against the small of her back. The railing wasn't very tall and over she went head first right into the water. Right into that spot."

Cham pointed at the area the gray cloud occupied.

"The water wasn't very deep and it was fairly calm that day, but she became trapped under the keel of the boat. She couldn't get to the surface even though she was only a few feet under water. She drowned. She drowned because her own child pushed her in the water."

Steven looked to the ground for a moment, steadied himself, and then bore back into Cham.

"Very sad story, but what does it have to do with me?"

"That woman still can't understand what happened. She can't comprehend why her boy pushed her, why she had to die that way. It's not right. It's not only a matter of accepting her death, it's accepting how she died. There was no justice in it, and deep down, you wonder the same thing."

"Like I've said, there's a great many things I wonder about, but that doesn't change anything."

"It does if you'll be honest with yourself. How does it make you feel to know a ten-year-old boy killed his own mother?"

"Terrible," was Steven's one-word response.

"And how do you think it made her feel?"

"I can't imagine."

"And what does it make you think of God?"

Steven steadied himself. "It doesn't change how I feel. Did you expect me to blame Him for that?"

"You used to."

"Maybe, but not anymore."

"Why not?"

"Because I don't know enough to place blame on anyone."

"Very nice answer, but look deeper. Don't you really want to know how something like that was even possible? A mother killed by her own son? How could a caring God let something like that happen?"

"Maybe it was an accident."

"An accident?" Cham exclaimed. "How can pushing someone over the side of a boat be an accident? I mean how does that figure? I can tell you in all honesty how it happened. I can see it just as I saw how you died in the flood. The boy snuck up behind her. He didn't want her to see him. He reached out with his hand and pressed against her back. That's not an accident. He didn't trip and fall into her. He didn't even run toward her calling her name so he could give her a hug. He reached out deliberately while making sure she didn't see him. How can that possibly be an accident?"

Steven would not answer.

"Maybe I'm not being totally fair," Cham offered in a conciliatory tone. "Maybe it was somewhat accidental. Perhaps the kid really didn't want to see her dead. Maybe he thought it would just be a grand joke to see her splash around in the water. And then what? Some poor kid that doesn't know any better shoves his mother into the water. Yeah, it's mean, but he didn't want to see it go beyond that. Doesn't matter. He saw her topple over and die regardless of what his intentions were. The kid would have to live with that for the rest of his life? Is that right?"

"I don't know what's right. I wasn't even there."

"Or maybe it really wasn't an accident at all. Maybe the kid hated his mother and did it to finally be rid of her. Maybe that's why he pushed her over. That would certainly explain why he tried to sneak up on her."

Once more, Steven said nothing.

"Or maybe the father told the kid to do it. Maybe good ol' dad wanted to be rid of his wife and convinced the kid to push mom in as some kind of joke. Only thing is, dad knew enough about boats that he was sure if she went over at the point she was standing, she wouldn't survive. He *knew* if he could convince the kid it was a harmless game to push his mother, the mother would most likely be dead. Maybe that's what happened . . . a father used his son as a weapon to kill his wife. How fair is that?"

Steven just looked out across the water at the gray mist and felt a great sadness pulling at his soul.

Cham fed that sorrow. "The problem for you is that you know all these things are possible. You've heard stories like this before. Husbands killing wives, mothers killing children, children killing parents, on and on it goes. You've read about terrible tragedies that made no sense, and all the time you wondered how such things could happen. Look at her, is it right that she waits out there for comprehension that is never going to come?"

"Like I said, I don't know what's right," Steven said flatly.

"You keep saying that, but isn't that why you shut the door on God?"

"What are you talking about?"

"I'm talking about the door that you now want to open. The problem for you is that you're the one that shut it. You shut that door—deep down you know that, don't you. Just admit it."

"Yes, I made the door, so I'm the one that shut it." Steven realized that had to be true. He knew he made the door and he knew he made it so it was shut. That, however, was when he first entered the afterlife, now he felt something different, and he exclaimed as much with absolute determination. "But now I want it opened. I don't want to be barred from God."

"Are you sure? You're standing here now sad, angry, and upset. Who are you angry at? Me? I don't think so. Are you mad at her?" Cham pointed to the essence of the woman in the river. "You're not mad at her. How could you be? But you're upset at someone. Who does that leave? Maybe you need to keep that door closed a bit longer until you can sort this all out, until you're ready to see a God that allowed things like this to happen, for a child to kill his mother."

"You're twisting things around."

"Am I? Or am I just making you face the things you've already thought about. Maybe I'm just saying what's already on your mind."

"You want me to admit it? Fine, there were times I didn't understand how such things were possible. I couldn't fathom the injustice of it all. Maybe I blamed God, but I never stopped believing."

"It doesn't matter whether or not you just believed He existed. Don't you think it's important how you saw Him? If you saw Him as unjust, then maybe you still have a few things to learn before you go barging in on Him."

"You want to convict me on having doubts, go ahead. I'm guilty as charged. But if you're saying I want to see God now just so I can blame him for everything bad that has happened, then you're dead wrong."

"I hope you're right about that, because if you're not then you will have to face those consequences we talked about." Cham nodded as if he was convinced he covered that topic sufficiently. He then moved on to the initial purpose of their visit to this place. "We've debated your intentions. We know the action you propose, now let's see about the consequences."

"Fine."

"Is it fine?" Cham countered. "You say you don't want to be separated from God, but at the same time, that is exactly what you risk. That's one of the pains you face. If God doesn't quite see things the way you do, He just might cast you out forever."

Cham pointed one last time to the gray mist in the water. "That woman out there, she didn't accept her death because she couldn't believe it was possible for the way she died. She saw no justice in that and who could blame her? A mother killed by her own child. There's too much pain there for her to even contemplate the existence of God, and so she rejected her own death. Now she is totally separated from God."

Cham turned his attention back to Steven.

"I'm telling you that you're risking the same thing. If you defy God, you risk being barred from Him forever. It won't be just a door that you create that separates you from Him, it will be a permanent barrier. You will become just like her. I think you should know how it feels."

"I can guess how it feels."

"Oh no, you can't, but I can show you. Go over to her now. Submerge yourself in the midst of her essence. Open yourself to her feelings, not just your own. This is a new perception for you, but it is certainly possible for you now. It's like reading her mind. She won't stop you. If anything, she'll invite you to share her agony."

Steven hesitated.

"I know you're not scared," Cham allowed. "I can't scare

you. The question is, do you really want to know? If you're so certain that you're right, what's the harm in seeing where it can lead only if you're wrong?"

There was truth in that. Why should Steven fear consequences he believed he would never face?

Steven willed himself forward. He did not step into the water. Instead, he floated just above the surface of the river. He kept a steady pace and a straight line. He did not want to frighten this lost spirit of a woman, but he intended on moving forward as directly as possible. He only stopped when he was but an arm's length from the gray haze.

He stood there silent for a moment, wondering what to do. He waited for the cloud to fling itself at him the way it attacked Cham on their previous visit to this place.

The mist did not move. The water, however, appeared to churn faster beneath it.

Finally, Steven made the first attempt to communicate.

"Hello, I'm Steven."

The gray haze did not respond.

"Do you have a name?"

A breeze from the center of the fog whispered the name to Steven.

"Laura."

"Hello, Laura."

At this point, Steven had no idea what to say next. He struggled for words that would not come easily.

"Is the water cold?"

"Yes . . . No. . . ."

"Why are you here?"

"I fell."

"Can I help you?"

"No."

"How long have you been here?"

"Not long, but the boat . . . it left."

"You're waiting for it to come back?"

"No . . . Yes. . . ."

"Maybe it won't come back. I mean maybe they don't know you fell."

"They know."

"How long are you going to wait?"

Silence.

"Are you hurt?" Steven asked without allowing the quiet to linger.

"Yes . . . No. . . ."

"And you're sure I can't help you?"

"I'm sure."

"Do you want to walk with me a bit? Maybe we can go over to the side of the river and wait there, or maybe we can go looking for the boat."

"No."

Steven looked to the river bank where Cham was waiting patiently.

"Listen, do you see that person standing there at the edge of the water?"

"Yes."

"Do you know him?"

"No."

"You attacked him not too long ago. Do you remember that?"

"Yes . . . No. . . ."

"If you remember him at all, can you tell me why you might have attacked him?"

"He lied."

For the first time since his death, Steven felt cold.

"He lied? About what?"

"About me."

This is not what Steven expected, but he pressed for details.

"You know what he said about you?"

"I heard."

"He told me you were pushed off the boat. . . ."

"I fell!"

"He told me you drowned."

"The boat left!"

"What do you remember?"

The gray mist moved quickly. The woman's essence encased Steven's form and the two were linked in thought.

The grayness of the fog covered Steven's vision. The world about him became fuzzy. Very quickly, even the water below him faded out of sight. At first, all he could perceive was the gray mist that surrounded him, but eventually scenes of the river returned to his mind.

What he saw, however, was not the river of the present, it was the past. Many more trees filled the edges of the banks on both sides. The lush thick leaves made a solid wall of green that could not be penetrated by his sight. There were no buildings anywhere to be seen, no bridges, and no roads. The birds sang clearer and louder. The current of the river ran stronger. There was not a single sign of man's presence anywhere, until he saw the boat.

Instantly, he found himself in the vessel. He stood upon a creaky wooden deck at the bow. A warm breeze filled his face, but it could not completely block out a displeasing smell he could not quite define. It was like rotten fish being burned with garbage and it made him queasy The wind, thankfully, helped ease any growing sickness.

He ventured a look down below him as well as behind. The hull appeared to have a shallow draft and it was in dire need of maintenance. What once was bright white had degraded into a patchwork of dark green, gray, and brown. If he leaned over the side, he could probably scrape off a pound of muck and slime with his bare hand just from where he stood.

Behind him, he saw the large rectangular cabin. A tall black smokestack rose out of the center of the blocky enclosure that offered shelter for the crew and other passengers. Dark smoke belched out of the top of the pipe in continuous but uneven puffs. He could not see the stern from where he stood, but he could hear the paddles smacking the water in a steady beat.

Returning his gaze to the river before him, he focused on the fresher air flowing around him. He did not mind the unsteady rock of the boat, but the lingering smell clearly offended him.

To his utter surprise, he felt a sharp shove on the small of his back. It lacked great force, but for some reason he could not fight off the push and he lost his balance. His thighs and knees hit a small railing in front of him which served to knock him from his feet. Tumbling over the top rail, he knew he was headed into the water below.

As he toppled head first with his feet up in the air, his face came back toward the boat and he could see what was once behind him. He saw a young boy with a grin on his face. Then he saw the dark stained wood of the boat's forward hull, then the water, and then darkness.

He felt pressure on his back and then in his chest. His head throbbed as if it was going to burst. He wanted to scream, but something held his mouth shut. The darkness that covered his vision turned purple, then red, then white. And with that, the pressure and pain suddenly disappeared.

He found himself standing in water up to his shoulders. He thought his feet stood planted in the soft river bed below, but he couldn't be sure. For some reason, the mud didn't feel as firm as it should. It was almost as if he was standing in whipped cream. His arms felt unsteady as well, as if they couldn't truly propel him through the water if he had to swim.

Uncertain of his movements, Steven simply watched the dark shadow of the boat now ahead of him drift away with a trail of black smoke lagging behind.

Wondering when the boat would turn around, Steven stood still in the water, waiting patiently at first. As the boat continued moving downstream, that patience quickly ebbed. He realized the boat was not making any attempt to turn around and retrieve him. In fact, it wasn't even slowing down.

His patience turned first into uncertainty and confusion. He could not understand why the boat wouldn't stop. He wondered if he should shout out or try to follow. Those sensations quickly gave way to anger as the boat became nothing more than a small speck in the distance. He knew he couldn't catch up now and so he stood there in the water, alone.

His anger did not grow. Instead, it became a slight seething bitterness he could almost taste. It remained just prevalent enough to make its presence known, but it did not turn into true rage.

He decided he would not shout for help, nor would he move from this spot. What happened to him was not his fault, it was not his doing, and he would not suffer for it. Eventually, those responsible would realize their error. They would come back, apologize for not keeping him safe and for leaving him there, leaving him alone in the water.

At this moment, he realized he was sensing exactly what Laura was feeling upon her death. She felt injured, discarded, and more importantly, abandoned. It was that emotion she could not ease, and it was that emotion that continued to grow.

The pain and resentment opened a hole in Steven's core as he felt every joyous hope and dream slip from his essence like hot oil down a candlestick. A shadow grew over his soul, and just as it darkened his spirit, it chased away all that was promising to a young life. Optimism gave way to pessimism, trust turned to cynicism, and hope shattered into despair.

And yet something else shadowed the recesses of his mind. Beyond the simmering anger and beneath the billowing sense of abandonment, the image of a young boy with a grin on his face latched onto his consciousness. This one reflection of the past haunted him like no other regret of his own ever could. The remorse of his own errors and flaws of his past life could crush his spirit if he allowed it, but even the summation of all his regrets could not match the grief encompassed in this one single memory.

Try as he might he could not shake the face of the grinning boy from his vision.

Why was he smiling?

Why did he push me?

Why Was He Smiling?

Why didn't he try to help me?

WHY WAS HE SMILING?

Why didn't he call for help?

WHY WAS HE SMILING? WHY WAS HE SMILING?

A lonely hollowness—an emptiness ten times the sensation Steven felt at the bare foundation of his old home—fell upon his form like a cloak of lead. The weight of this sorrow brought him out of the past and into the present, for it was the despair that blossomed over a century of waiting.

The river was now once again as he used to remember it—the trees not as thick, the current not as quick. Once more, he saw Cham on the river bank. He realized this is what Cham wanted him to feel, this overwhelming sorrow. The emptiness inside this woman was as vast as anything he could describe.

Steven called out, but not to Cham for help. He called out to the woman tormented for years upon years.

"He didn't understand. Your boy, he couldn't have. It was a game to him, that's all."

"My boy?"

"It was your boy that pushed you."

"I fell!"

"It doesn't have to be this way. You don't have to keep torturing yourself. It happened. It was a terrible mistake, but it happened. Nothing can change that. If you just accept. . . ."

"I won't . . . I can't"

"Yes, you can. It happened. I don't know why, but it did, but you don't have to live with it forever."

"They will come back."

"No, they won't. Everyone on that boat is dead. Your husband is dead, the captain of the boat is dead, the crew is dead, the passengers are dead. Your boy is dead. They're all dead."

Silence.

"Look around you. What do you see? Where are the riverboats? They don't come around anymore. There are boats now, but they're different, faster. It's been years since you fell. More years than you can count. How many times did you see the seasons change? How long have you been here? Who could possibly live that long?"

The gray mist moved off of Steven's form as if in retreat. The emptiness lifted from Steven as she left, but Steven would not give up.

"Count back, you know it's a long time. More than a hundred years. They couldn't be alive."

"I haven't left. I'm still here."

"That's because you're waiting for something that can't possibly happen."

"Go away."

"Maybe we can move on together."

"Go away."

"I don't want to leave you here."

"Go away."

"Can't you just give me a chance to show you?"

"Go away."

With that, Steven knew the futility of his situation. She would now only repeat those two words, nothing else. He turned and willed himself back to Cham's side.

"So now you know how she feels," Cham said with no hint of satisfaction.

"Yes, I know."

"She's separated herself from God, but that only gives you a taste of what you face. She still doesn't believe she's dead, so the sorrow she feels is tempered by that fact. You, on the other hand, you understand your situation quite clearly. If you are cast out, you won't be able to deny it like her. You won't be able to hide from the truth, or fool yourself into hoping that something will save you in the future. There will be no hope. You'll have to face every instant of your existence with that understanding for eternity."

"Not a pleasant thought," Steven admitted.

"It wasn't meant to be."

"But in the end, it doesn't really matter?"

"Doesn't matter? How can you say that?" Cham questioned with a baffled expression.

"By showing me this, you didn't convince me to stay away from the door. If anything, it did the opposite. It's shown me that the longer I'm separated from God, the worse off I'm going to be. If I just accept indifference now, it will become a part of me, it will take over. And then I really won't have a future or past. It won't matter what kind of dream I create. I won't care about anything, and then I really will be just like her."

Cham became almost belligerent in facing Steven's refusal. "You can twist this anyway you want, but it still comes down to you forcing yourself on God. You're going to throw open that door whether He wants you to or not. You're doing it because you want to."

"That's right. I do want to. I'm not supposed to be separated from God. Like you said, I put that door there, and that means I'm the one that has to open it."

Cham was silent for a moment as a frown crossed his lips. He shook his head with dissatisfaction.

"Okay, you've seen sorrow and that hasn't convinced you. Now you need to see what else hell has in store. Fear and helplessness."

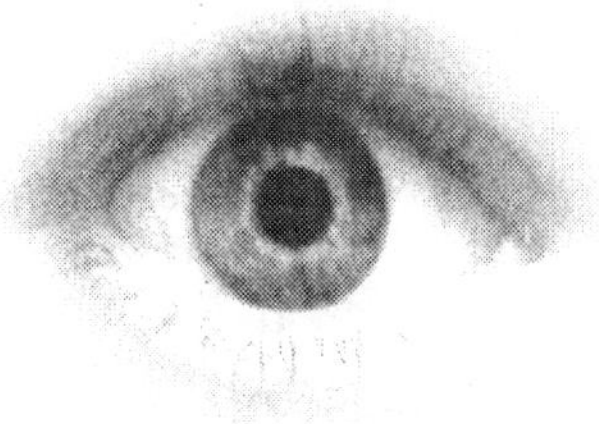

SUFFERING

"It's funny. Everyone thinks the spider is always the monster. You know, haunted houses, scary movies, they all show the spider as the terrible creature that preys on everything else. It's not always true."

"We're going to talk about spiders?" Steven asked in an obvious state of incomprehension.

"We're going to talk about fear and helplessness," Cham shot back as if the question was almost insulting. "That's another part of the consequences you face. When you walk into hell, you don't get to experience the good things in life. You get the bad things, and the insect world is the perfect illustration of that."

Steven was at a total loss. His conversations with Cham were becoming more and more surreal. He could not imagine how insects could possibly have anything to do with the decision he faced.

"But I'm not a bug."

"You're not a bug right now, but you obviously have no idea what might happen to you in hell. Can you tell me with certainty what hell is like?"

"Of course not."

"Then allow me to continue," Cham demanded.

"Fine, I'll listen to what you have to say about spiders and insects, but just so you know, I'm not going to keep this up forever."

Cham's eyes opened a little wider as if surprised by this statement. "But you now have forever. You're not on the clock anymore. You don't have a mortal body that's going to expire."

"What I mean is that I'm allowing you to show me this so you understand I'm not dismissing you completely. I acknowledge you're here for some reason, a reason that right now I can't comprehend, but I won't deny that somehow you're here because I've allowed it. You helped me for a while, but now I think you're possibly more of a hindrance, and I really don't think you understand me anymore. I've listened to your arguments and heard what you've had to say. I'm convinced now more than ever that I need to open that door. I'm not going to be separated from God much longer."

"You've been back on earth only for a short while and already you're losing patience? Perhaps you haven't advanced as far as I thought."

"I have no idea what you thought," Steven countered, "but this is not about patience. It's about giving you a fair chance to speak your mind, but I can't simply follow you around from one place to another with no end in sight. I mean right now you're talking about spiders and insects. I have no idea where you could possibly be going with this, but I know there are about a zillion different types of bugs. If we're going to talk about each one, then that in itself could go on forever. At some point, I'm going to view this as just stalling."

"I have no intention of stalling, and I don't want to talk about all the different types of bugs. This won't take long at all. In fact, this is the last thing I want to show you. As long as you truly listen to what I have to say and follow what I ask you to consider, we can go back to the room you made and you can make your own decision on what to do about that door."

"Fair enough, what do you want me to do?"

"First, I want you to think about life for a moment. Not your old life, not the afterlife you might think is ahead of you, but life here on earth where you think God doesn't exist."

"I thought God existed everywhere," Steven shot back as if he was prepared to challenge anything Cham stated.

"I don't want to get in a philosophical argument about that now. As you might say, it's a waste of time. I'm just trying to give you an idea of what hell might be like for you. In order for you appreciate that, you have to be able to consider a place where there is no God. Previously, a true understanding of that might have been beyond your comprehension, but not anymore. Now that your perception has grown, you can get a taste of hell without actually going there."

"And this is the last thing you want to show me? You want to scare me to a point that I'll be too afraid to open the door."

"No, not to scare you, but to enlighten you. I want you to see the world as it is. I still believe you have your doubts and that these doubts are feeding your emotions more than you will admit. Just like with the woman in the river, there are two things you need to face—what are your true feelings about God and what is it like to truly suffer."

Steven remained combative. "Facing those things before didn't change my mind, so I think you're just wasting your time."

"Humor me."

" Okay I'm willing to give you this one last chance."

"Great, then think about this. There are creatures on earth that get a really raw deal. Insects, for example, don't experience much in their life. All that pretty much motivates them is fear and hunger and some strange desire to make more little bugs. They live in constant fear of being eaten in a way that's pretty much too horrible to conceive. At the same time, they hunt around for food wondering where their next meal is going to come from. That's there entire life summed up swiftly but accurately."

"I get it," Steven admitted. "The insect world is pretty barbaric. Most of nature is that way. It's eat or be eaten and it's a cruel world. If you're just going to go through that again, you're wasting your time. I've already told you, I don't understand why the world is the way it is, but I'm not going to blame God for it."

"You admitted before that you use to."

"Yes, I did, but even before I died, I stopped that. I can't blame anyone for things I can't possibly understand, especially God. It didn't make sense then and it doesn't make sense now."

"You say that now, but maybe you can get a better understanding of things by truly experiencing what fear and helplessness are all about, and what better way to do that than to see what life is like in the insect world."

Life in the insect world? Was Cham serious?

"I have to tell you, this is all very bizarre. I want to give you a chance, but I'm not making a connection here. How is understanding bugs going to change my perception?"

"Not just change, but enhance. I keep telling you that you're risking something very dangerous, but just telling you this is obviously not enough. You're going to have to see for yourself what consequences await you. Once you get a glimpse of what I have to show you, you will face two questions. The first is whether or not you still have removed all your doubts about God, and the second is whether you really want to risk a fate that is worse than what you are about to experience."

Steven simply shrugged. "And it's obvious to me that you're not going to accept my word that I don't have any doubts about what I'm supposed to do and that I'm not afraid of hell. Let's just get this over with. What is it we need to do?"

Cham turned about and peered deep into the trees. After long moments of focus, he nodded his head in satisfaction.

"Found one. It should be perfect, but we have to move fast. Come with me."

Cham flew off in a blur deep into the trees and Steven had to will himself forward as fast as he could concentrate in order to keep up. When Cham came to a sudden stop, Steven almost flew by him.

Floating in the air next to a large elm tree, Steven pulled beside Cham.

"Why did you stop here?"

Cham pointed to a nearby branch. "Do you see that spider?"

"Yes."

"It's a common jumping spider," Cham explained. "It catches its prey by pouncing on its victims as opposed to snaring them in a web. It's a nasty looking creature to be sure, and usually it's the predator, but I don't think that will be the case today."

Cham then nodded to a winged insect on several branches above the spider. "Do you also see that wasp? It's clinging to a branch next to its nest. The nest is that long slender cylinder made of mud that's stuck on the trunk of the tree. Do you see it?"

"Yes, I see the bug and the nest."

"That's a dirt-dauber wasp."

"Looks like a regular old wasp to me."

"These wasps eat spiders and if I'm right it's going to spot that jumping spider any second. This is going to happen fast, so you can't question me on this. Otherwise, you're going to have to wait until we find another situation like this. If you want this to be over with quickly, then do exactly as I say."

"Fine"

"In your current state, you can join your thoughts with the spider. You don't have to make physical contact with it. You just have to allow your essence to mix with that of the spider. Remember, you don't have a physical form. You are now a purely spiritual being. All you have to do is project yourself to link with the physical presence of the spider. Do you understand what I'm talking about?"

Steven actually did understand. His own insight was indeed

growing. He knew the form of his body was nothing more than an illusion and that his true essence was not physical in any way. The limits that existed on his once mortal body were now removed and he could experience situations on an entirely new level.

"Yes, I understand."

"Then do it now, and don't break the link with the spider until its life is over. Trust me, that won't be long."

Steven did not like this idea at all, yet he did not hesitate for one moment. With a determination to keep to his word as well as a desire to hold Cham to his, he willed his own spiritual essence to join with the spider on the branch.

The connection became complete instantly as Steven's form disappeared from the trees past the river's shore. He was no longer on the outside simply observing the spider, he was now inside the arachnid, his essence linked to everything the spider was.

At once, the very substance of existence changed for Steven in ways that go far beyond human understanding. The stimulus of senses that assaulted his perception raged through him like static electricity building into one massive charge. It was as if every grain of his being was thrown into a state of monumental vigilance. Never before in his life had he ever felt so alert, and yet this did not fully describe the sensations coursing through his consciousness. It was as if all the possible dangers he ever faced were suddenly thrust upon him a thousand times over.

In the very instant his own awareness joined with the consciousness of the spider, it seemed as if there was no possible way to avoid calamity. If he stood still, he would be overcome. If he moved forward carefully, great harm would snatch him from behind. And if he fled, he would only race into a worse catastrophe.

Panic could only mildly describe this sensation, for it went far beyond any dread he ever experienced. Panic overwhelms conscious thought to a potential point of ruinous behavior. This unyielding alarm that flowed through every aspect of his consciousness remained at such a pitched level that panic was no longer a viable alternative, for it would only feed his heightened state of complete apprehension. All he could do was accept that danger was everywhere and realize that avoiding it was like dodging saltwater at the bottom of the ocean.

The link between Steven and the spider became so strong that his perception of the world matched that of his new host. He sensed everything the spider sensed—saw what it saw and felt what it felt. It went beyond a simple link of thoughts or a joining of senses. In many ways, Steven became one with the spider. Though he had no true control over the arachnid's movements, in every other way, he was the spider.

Steven's own awareness of the world around him altered itself to match the physical traits of the arachnid. He could see in several different directions at once. It was disorienting, until he realized he was now looking through eight eyes instead of two. The heightened visual ability did little to calm his sense of impending disaster. Even as he could see so much more of his surroundings, he felt vulnerable to threats he could not even identify. Even though he did not know what to fear, that fear existed at every point of focus.

He felt the jittering yet swift movements of the deft spider as if they were his own. He twisted and turned to inspect every conceivable angle. He moved with speed beyond his comprehension. The pouncing, darting, and spinning motions were so quick that Steven could barely associate intended movements of the spider's body with the motions he could sense. It was like involuntarily dancing to music with a beat twenty times faster than normal. It was very much as if he moved not by conscious decision but by some preordained pattern that might increase his chances of survival.

Once Steven attuned himself to the physical abilities of the spider, another overwhelming desire flooded his thoughts. He was hungry and he wanted food, badly.

Never in his life had he felt such a need. It drove him beyond the fear. It forced him onward. Such was this driving force that he knew he could not remain still. He would have to press on until he found sustenance.

The conflict of these desires was near maddening. All encompassing concern for his very existence kept him on constant guard, and yet, the festering hunger demanded he disregard his fear in order to search for food. These two forces battled for control with no clear victor. Just as Steven was overcome by the need to check every possible area for impending doom, he quickly felt the stinging pang of hunger force him to look for prey. Back and forth it went, and Steven felt like a mere puppet controlled by strings of dread and strings of starvation.

Steven did not see the dirt-dauber wasp until it landed upon him. As he felt the grip of insect legs take hold of his body, his hunger dissolved and fear took sole control, turning into a frenzy of self-preservation. Survival was now his only goal and he felt the spider fight with every ounce of its existence.

Steven could not truly follow the movements—which were in essence now his own—with any degree of comprehension as everything turned into the chaos of frenzied aggression. The actions Steven could distinguish were nothing more than jumbled rotations and lunges. He knew the spider was trying desperately to turn its fangs upon its attacker while trying to avoid the wasp's stinger. In the end, the spider failed on both counts.

Steven felt searing physical pain for only a split instant. Then, he lost contact with the spider's body. It was as if he now floated in nothingness while retaining a link to the spider's consciousness. The highly agitated movements ceased immediately just as the spider went limp, completely paralyzed by the wasp's venom.

Unable to resist in anyway, the spider now became nothing more than baggage for the wasp, and the winged insect took greater hold of the arachnid. Steven could no longer feel the grip of the wasp's legs but he could sense himself being propelled upward as the wasp took many short flying leaps with the spider in its clutches.

While he could no longer sense the body of the spider in any way, he still maintained the vantage point of the spider's eight eyes. The link between the two remained strong and the spider's limited understanding of its own predicament became Steven's clear focus.

The heightened instinctive alarm Steven felt when he first joined with the spider now turned to a frantic realization of impending disaster. All of the fear that rested instinctively within the spider, the impulses which made it acutely aware of so many possible dangers, swept over its limited awareness like a raging flood of seething passions. If fear were a drink, its taste would be acidic, and through his link with the spider, Steven's mouth burned with the flavor.

This extreme dread was matched only by the absolute helplessness of being unable to resist in anyway. It was one thing to panic at the outset of catastrophe, it was another thing entirely to be placed in disaster's path, staked to the ground and incapable of escape. Helplessness is an anchor tied to a calamity, and the spider was now clearly tied to a terrible fate it could not escape.

Steven was not completely unfamiliar with this feeling, only the magnitude. Still, there had been times in his life when devastation struck and he felt helpless to combat it. When tragedy occurs in whatever form and when unfortunate events trigger a crushing sense of despair, everything seems to spiral out of control. This is the feeling Steven had dreaded most in life and it now struck at him a thousand times over. The tension squeezed his soul as if it would press it down into nothingness. He wanted to scream with fury, to smash his fist against some hard unforgiving object—he needed to do something to release the frustration, but of course he could do nothing. Steven could not imagine a more consuming set of circumstances, and unfortunately, it was about to get much worse.

Eventually, the dirt-dauber wasp reached the entrance of its nest. It was a dark opening, like a long narrow cave that sank into the emptiness of despair. Steven knew the spider did not want to go into this hole, and thus he did not want to be dragged into this opening, either. It smelled of death, but there was nothing he could do. It was the worst of all possible nightmares—the inability to move, the complete lack of control, the dark and foreboding place, the suffocating enclosure of a coffin, all seasoned with monsters and the ultimate unknown demise.

The light ebbed as the spider was hauled into its final resting place, and at first, Steven saw nothing, but he heard a strange continuous crunching that sounded like the grinding of dry leaves through a shredder. Eventually, the spiders eyes grew accustomed to the darkness, and through its eyes, Steven could see the final horror that waited in this chamber.

A wasp larva nestled at the end of the hollow was already gnawing on a slightly-chewed, now half-dead spider of similar size, and it became clear to Steven that the same fate now waited for him.

Time seemed to inch by as Steven could only watch the larva complete its first meal. When that spider was done, it would be his turn. He wondered if the paralyzing venom of the wasp sting would keep him from feeling the torturous pain of being eaten alive. In truth, he didn't hold to much hope in this thought. Even if he could not sense the physical agony, he would not be able to avoid the mental devastation of watching himself being devoured piece by piece by this disgusting creature.

This might have been nature, but it was not pretty. It was gruesome in its harshness. The wait was torment. At times, Steven wished the creature would quickly finish off the other spider, so that his time in this chamber of terror would be limited as much as possible. Then, he would hope the monster might choke on its other dinner and perhaps give him a chance at escape.

While time might have seemed to tick by as if slowed by some unseen hand of gleeful evil, in reality the larva finished the first spider in short order and without hesitation began feasting on the leg of its next meal.

Thankfully, Steven could not feel the physical pain, but he could not remove his sight from the macabre scene. The mental anguish was beyond description and he almost wished he could feel the stinging bite of the larva to take his mind from this nightmare vision. He knew it was not his limb that was being devoured, but the link remained so strong between him and the spider, he could not separate himself from the spider's demise.

When the larva chewed up the leg and took hold of the spider's body with its jaws, Steven sensed one last crushing spasm of upheaval, and then the world went dark once more.

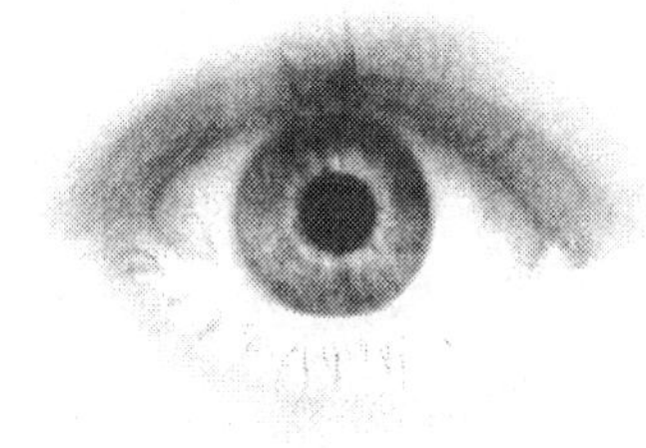

FAITH

Steven found himself back in the empty room with the single closed door that barred him from God. It was just like when he died in the flood. He simply appeared in the center of this vacant area the instant the larva tore open the spider's body. It was not a true physical existence he experienced while linked to the arachnid, even though it surely felt like one. Still, the results of death appeared to be the same. He was thrust into the spiritual space of the afterlife with no fanfare as his imagination recreated the clean, empty room as a sanctuary for his spirit.

His own form had returned to that of a human body, the body he had back in his previous life. Once more, he felt great freedom in his movements, a sensation he relished after being caught in the clenches of a predator.

The distress and helplessness he experienced in the last moments he lived as a spider evaporated from him without effort. At first, he welcomed the lack of any sensation. The nightmare he experienced was thankfully over and he faced no residual effects. Unlike his life back on earth where he would wake from a nightmare still shaking, still panicked, and restless over the experience, a steady calm flowed over his consciousness almost instantaneously.

The horrific encounter, however, remained trapped in his memory. Despite the fact the images would not elicit any degree of anxiety, he could not wipe them clean from his thoughts. He recalled them all very clearly, and the experience remained fresh and crisp as if he had truly lived the life of an insignificant creature that met a very disturbing end. This is not something he would ever wish to experience again, and he believed that acknowledgment is exactly what Cham desired.

The thought of Cham forced Steven about, and as he scanned the room, he heard footsteps coming up a set of stairs to his left. Steven watched silently as Cham moved confidently forward.

Regarding Steven with a probing look, Cham didn't blink as he stared deep into Steven's eyes. As if drinking in Steven's thoughts, a smile of satisfaction crossed Cham's lips. He looked like a prosecuting attorney that just gained a hard fought guilty verdict.

"Not a pleasant experience, was it?" Cham asked.

"No, not at all." Steven replied without debate, but he knew that victory was not Cham's.

"Sorry about that, but you needed to understand," Cham offered, almost sounding apologetic, but certainly carrying an air of vindication.

Steven decided to let some air out of that confident bubble. "Understand what? Understand that the life of a bug is far from one I would crave? You showed me that being an insect is harsh. Is that really such a major admission? I could have told you that without going through any of this."

Cham's eyes narrowed to focus on the growing resistance he received from Steven. He would not allow Steven to brush this lesson aside. He would hammer the point home if need be. "Yes, but you did go through it so you would know what it was like. Is it something you would want to go through again?"

"No," Steven admitted.

"Then now you understand what the consequences might be for making a terrible mistake. I didn't want to torture you, but you needed to see what hell is like. What you went through back there, that's just a fraction of it. Imagine going through something like that over and over again for all eternity. That's what I want you to get from all of this."

Steven, however, did not care what Cham wanted. Instead, he remained steadfast on doing the right thing. While it was indeed easy to bury his emotions in this place, it was not what he would accept. He would have to trust his instincts as well as his beliefs, and he could not do that if he simply found it much simpler to sink into absolute numbness.

Despite the fact he now understood what barbaric levels of torment existed and how they could haunt his view of reality, he forced his emotions free of the buffers that blocked them. He battled against the indifference and pushed away the apathy. He would allow the full breadth of his emotions, instincts, and character to rise up and be heard during this fateful moment.

He steadied himself instinctively as he half expected to resume the nightmare and crumble to the ground in despair, but he did not. He felt no terror and suffered from no pain. He did not relive the horror of his last experience as he pressed himself to gauge his feelings even deeper. What he did sense surprised him.

At that moment, the door in the distance called to him ever stronger. He could not deny the sensation. Like a magnet drawing iron, the barrier between him and God would not allow him to stand in reserve, to wait for some new sign. In fact, he no longer considered the door a barrier, but more of an opportunity. Throwing it open would prove his faith, and crossing the threshold stood out as a beacon of a new beginning.

"I'm sorry," Steven began, "but you didn't get what you wanted. You might have showed me what hell is like, but you haven't changed my mind."

Amazingly, Cham looked away. He turned his back on Steven even as he made one last attempt to dissuade him from making a serious error.

"Really? Perhaps you're not giving this a true chance to sink in." Cham then paused only for a moment, as if to let Steven contemplate the fallacy of his plans. Then, he made his final argument. "I'm sorry to hear you won't listen to reason. I've showed you what you might be in for, but only in the most basic sense. What you went through is just the smallest slice of the whole pie you're about to eat. The torment of the lost soul, the helplessness of the spider—hell is that kind of anguish a thousand times over and repeated again, and again, and again. It won't end. You won't get to come back here for some kind of break. You'll go from one horrendous situation to one that is worse."

"It doesn't matter."

"How can you say it doesn't matter?" Cham demanded. "I just showed you two examples, just two! I could have showed you hundreds . . . thousands. I could have showed you pain you couldn't believe. I just gave you a glimpse."

"Trust me, it was enough. More wouldn't have helped your cause."

"Are you really forgetting the woman in the river? Have you disregarded her emptiness? I know you aren't forgetting the spider's fate. Are you willing to relive that kind of torment for all eternity?"

Steven saw his own reality. He knew there was pain in the world. He knew there was suffering. He still didn't understand it all, but he knew—with all his soul—he knew he could not let that deter him from God. If he did, then he truly was opening a door, but not the one that blocked him from God. Instead, he would be flinging open the one that led to his own personal hell.

"Are you asking me if I understand that's what could happen to lost souls? Yes, I understand that completely. Do I think I'm really risking that? Only if I stay here and wait, then I am risking something terrible. That's really the choice here, to move forward and open that door or wait for something that's never going to happen."

Cham would not relent. He twirled about and pointed an angry finger directly at Steven. He spelled out his own viewpoint in cold contrast. "Let me tell you what will happen, then. You still have your doubts. That's really what caused you so much torment. It wasn't the spider being eaten by a wasp or some poor woman being pushed in a river by her son. It was about how God could let those things happen. I couldn't have brought you to those things if you didn't allow it. You wanted me to show you those things because it reaffirms your own questions."

Steven didn't know if Cham was finally telling the whole truth or if this was one last ploy to change his decision, but he could not deny the facts these words held.

"You're saying I wanted you to show me those terrible things?" Steven asked.

"Yes, you did," Cham insisted, and this point would not go unexplained. Cham would drive it home. "I follow your lead, not the other way around. I could only come in here when you accepted your death. I can only show you the things you are willing to see. You may not know what I'm talking about, but you will. You will when you open up that door and face God. All the truth will come out, and when it does you'll have to face the consequences."

Steven suddenly felt unsure of himself again. The room seemed to grow larger, but emptier at the same time, and the door seemed to move much further away. It still called to him, but he could not deny the call grew fainter.

Cham continued with fury. "Do you understand what this means? I'm not the one trying to convince you of something. I'm not fighting to change your mind. I'm just pointing out what's already inside you. How many times have you really wondered how God could possibly exist? How many times?"

"More than I would like to say," Steven admitted.

"And you don't think He knows that? You think you can hide that from Him?"

"I don't want to hide anything."

"We both know that's not even remotely true. You want to hide from the truth! I didn't show you anything you didn't want to see. Actually, nothing I showed you was even new to you. You always saw pain and suffering in the world around you. You focused on it. You dwelled on it. And you blamed God for it!"

"We've gone through this," Steven acknowledged. "I've already admitted this, but I don't blame Him anymore."

"No? Then why did I show you what it's like to be a helpless spider?"

"Because you're trying to change my mind."

"I got the spider from you! Don't you understand that yet? I pulled it from your memories, from your doubts."

"That may very well be true."

"Then you admit it. You still have your doubts."

"I admit it's about doubt, but not the way you're describing." Steven fought through the haze that was clouding his judgment, which was pressing his desire to be with God aside. He focused on the one truth he knew was the key. "It's about defeating those doubts. It's about faith. You want me to give in to my doubts, to simply accept them and then wait for God to tell me it's alright. I don't think it works that way. I think it's up to me to have enough faith just to believe."

"Believe in what? Believe in a God that would allow for such torment to exist? Isn't that what this is really about? Think back and take a good hard look at what you remember about life on earth. There was pain, there was fear, there was injustice, and there was helplessness. Why? How could a caring God even exist when He allows such things? When you open that door, you'll come face to face with everything you ever questioned about life. If God is capable of creating a world that is filled with so much suffering, then just think what fate awaits you when you decide to really face Him. You're going to want to ask Him why, and when you do, you'll also be telling Him you know better. That's when your trouble will really begin."

Steven shook his head as if to release cobwebs from his face. The haze was lifting. The picture was becoming clearer to him now and he knew what he had to do. "You're wrong about that. If I still blamed God for all the misery back on earth, then I wouldn't want to see Him now. Your own argument doesn't even make sense to me anymore. It might have once, but not now. I'm sorry but I've had enough of this. I'm going to open that door, and there's nothing you can do to stop me."

"You still won't listen to reason?"

"I disagree, I am listening to reason, my own reasons. I will not bury what's really inside of me and that's what you want me to do. That's what I would have to do to stay here. I'm not even sure where *here* is, and that's something else that just dawned on me. When you first showed up, I asked you if this was heaven and you didn't answer. Now I think I know why. It might seem like heaven where you can make almost any dream come to life, but what's heaven without God? That's why you wouldn't answer me, isn't that right?"

Cham said nothing.

"Is this heaven?"

Silence.

"It can't be, can it? It can't be because God's not here and there can't be heaven without God. That's the first answer I've come across that I truly understand. So there it is. This isn't heaven, so why would I want to stay here? I wouldn't. I would want to move on."

Cham still would not relinquish in this battle of wills. "But you still have your doubts about God. Congratulations, maybe you've figured out the truth about heaven, but it doesn't solve your dilemma with God."

"What dilemma is that?"

"Why does God allow it to happen? Why does a woman get pushed off a boat by her son and then have to live through eternity in torment? Why is nature so cruel that even insignificant creatures such as spiders suffer such a life of torment? Why? That is where your doubt lies. It goes beyond doubt. You *want* to blame God. Even now! That is *why* you closed that door when you came into this afterlife. I didn't do it, God didn't do it. You did it, and now you have to face why!"

Steven fought back just as hard. "You know what? You're right. I did close it. God didn't close it. I did. And it doesn't matter *why*, it just means it's up to me to open it. That's now the second answer I've come across. God's not here, but if I want to get to Him, I have to have faith. I may not know everything there is to know about life *or death*, but I have learned a few things. I'm realizing that some things you have to take on trust. Maybe the answers aren't always clear, maybe I'm not supposed to understand why things are the way they are. I just have to trust what's inside, and what's inside me tells me that waiting around is not the answer. I can't wait for God to open the door. I have to do it."

"Is that your decision?" Cham asked in near disbelief.

"It is."

"Well, good luck to you, but don't say I didn't warn you."

Steven turned away from Cham and toward the door. As he did, he revealed his own understanding. "It's not about luck."

He walked to the door and placed his hand on the knob. He stood at the door and said more to himself, "It's about faith. That's the one thing my wizard friend forgot. Intentions, actions, consequences . . . and *faith*. I just have to believe." He then turned the knob with great anticipation and threw open the door.

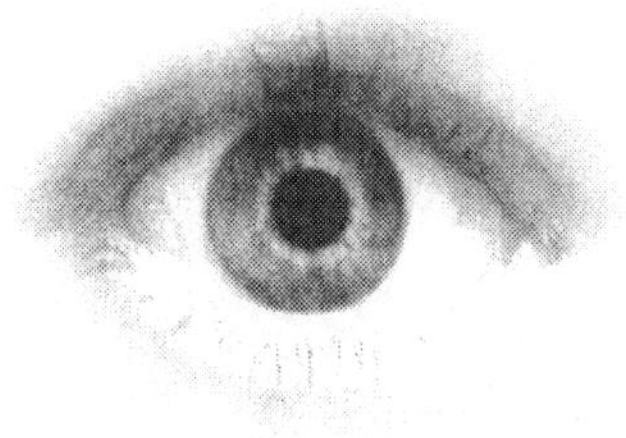

PERSISTENCE

The very instant Steven opened the door, the knob disintegrated in his hand and the entire door faded away before him as if it was never there. The stark, white walls and the plain, slate-like floor disappeared as well, all of it replaced by a new and glorious world.

Just as when he initially passed over to this new spiritual plane, the opening of the door signaled yet another transformation to the very core of his existence. This change, however, was not so subtle. He remained a spiritual being with the same identity and memories he cultivated on earth, but the barriers he constructed between him and heaven, between him and God, were now gone. He stepped into this new existence with exuberance.

While he could not feel the hands of angels lifting him to the heavens, his soul seemed to soar with joy. He did not hear a heavenly choir welcoming him with some grand hymn, but the sound of peace soothed his troubled spirit. And while he didn't stand before a golden city in the clouds, for him, what appeared all about was just as magnificent.

This was not a place of indifference and emptiness, nor was

it a breeding ground for conflicting emotions and uncertainty. Happiness and cheer filled this new world around him, and it showered him with the warmth of acceptance.

He saw before him his old house, the one swept away by the flood, except now it was whole once more, returned to a pristine state. To see it completely restored, he realized how much he loved it, how much it meant to him. That house represented his home, and that's where he truly was now—home.

Marveling at everything about him, he looked up into a clear blue sky dotted with white clouds that seemed to dance with freedom. On the distant horizon, he looked upon the majestic outline of towering mountains. He never lived near mountains, though he always wished to. Still, these mountains appeared familiar, and then he recalled where he had seen them before. This magnificent range of peaks matched what he created in his fantasy story with Roan. His smile broadened and his contentment blossomed.

Just like near his home back on earth, there were trees filling the grounds in every direction, but the trees that adorned this landscape appeared larger and healthier than the ones he remembered, and they stood just as regal as the mountains in the distance. Birds and squirrels filled the branches, and they welcomed Steven with enthusiastic chirps and whistles.

The warmth that filled him, the blue skies that greeted him, and the animals that welcomed him, all of this made him realize instantly there was no mistake in throwing open that door. There would be no punishment for his actions. No, he was truly where he belonged and his own essence glowed like a bright star in a clear winter's night sky.

He looked at his own hands, his own body, and he realized his imagination was once again filling the space around him. It gave his essence form and created the wonderful sanctuary around him. In one way, it was as if opening the door changed little. He knew he could make every dream come true in this place just as he could before, but there was much more to it than that.

As he basked in the warmth that surrounded him, he realized something else. There truly was no emptiness here, no indifference like the apathy which enveloped him when he first entered the empty room of his afterlife. In this place, he was no longer alone, not anymore. There was no closed door that blocked him from God—or God from him. God was in this space with him. He could feel it, the acknowledgement was beyond doubt. It filled him with hope and restored his belief in all that was right, just and good.

He didn't have to hear a voice; he didn't have to see some grand figure in flowing robes. Steven sensed God's existence everywhere. It could not be denied. Steven's spiritual energy did not simply fill empty space. Instead, his essence mixed with the mighty presence of God. This is what opening the door allowed.

He realized now that Cham's warnings were as hollow as his own doubts. There was never any risk of being cast into hell; such a thing could not happen to those that truly seek God. That was his true intention, that is what fueled his actions, and for that, there would be no grave consequences. There would only be the rewards of heaven. By throwing open that door, he did in fact surrender to his own faith and that faith had brought him home and more.

As a simple gesture of his own acceptance, Steven willed his form into the air above his house and he flew with the birds in the trees. The freedom and joy he felt at this moment went far beyond what he encountered the first time he flew when he returned to earth with Cham. This time he flew with God, and he knew the feeling would go on for as long as he wished. There was truly no fear here, no regret, and no sadness.

The birds acknowledged his presence as they joined him in the air. Together they darted back and forth, swooping through the trees and then high in the air. From that vantage point,

Steven could see all the way to the mountains and nothing ever looked so beautiful.

When he returned his gaze back to his house, he saw a figure standing on the front porch. With a simple twist, Steven soared back to the ground and landed but a few steps away from this unannounced visitor.

"Hello," a man with a wide smile offered. "Welcome home."

"Hi there!" Steven said joyously because he knew, in fact, he was finally home. Steven looked closer at his guest and suddenly recognized him. This was not a creation of his imagination, but the actual spirit of a grandfather he never got the chance to meet in his previous life.

"I know you," Steven stated confidently. "We're related. You're my grandfather."

"That's right. Thrilled to finally meet you. My name is Vic."

The man held out his hand, which Steven took and shook firmly. Strong emotions filled Steven. This man before him had nothing but love for Steven and it shone brightly the moment the two touched. Not only was God with him, he had family here as well.

"You died before I was born," Steven stated. "I never met you, but I know you."

"Yep, the truth is as plain as my face here. I couldn't lie to you if I wanted to. 'Course, I don't want to, but you know that, too."

"You're right. I can see the truth here. I am in heaven. It's not even a question anymore. I don't have to ask where I am. I don't have to ask for confirmation. I know. I'm where I belong."

"Yes you are, but truth be told, I wasn't sure if you were going to make it here."

Steven's thoughts raced back to the turmoil he faced with Cham. Just as Vic had claimed, the truth was clear and Steven knew what his grandfather meant.

"You wondered if I was going to be able to open that door.

You thought the doubt might be too great. It almost was, but it didn't stop me. Still, you were worried about me."

"Worried isn't probably the right word for it, but I couldn't tell for sure how it was going to turn out," Vic admitted. "You never can until the decision is made, and that decision was always totally up to you. You went through a pretty big struggle there, harder than I ever expected."

Steven acknowledged his own understanding. "Cham was pretty serious about keeping me from here, wasn't he?"

"Yes, but there's another truth deep inside. You just have to look for it."

"Something else about Cham?" Steven asked.

"Yes. It may not be clear to you yet, because you're not all the way here."

"What do you mean?"

"You've proved to yourself that you accept God, that's how you got here, but you also have to understand *why* it took so long for you to get here."

This time, the truth did not come easy. Steven fought through a fog, a puzzle of his own making, but eventually, he started to recognize the pieces. The first piece became quite clear as Steven dwelled on a fact he could not deny.

"Cham came from inside me, but that's not all," Steven said knowingly. A glimpse of the acknowledgment turned into a revelation. "Even more so than Roan, Cham was really me. He wasn't some outsider trying to help me. He was the part of me that was afraid to believe. I gave into those doubts when I created him, just like when I created the door. Cham represented my fears about God, and through him, I held to those fears even after I died."

Vic simply agreed. He could do nothing else. "That's certainly part of it. Cham was the part of you that didn't want to trust in God. He was pretty much everything that got you sent to earth in the first place. You'll understand all of that soon enough."

The other puzzle pieces seemed to shift. Were they all there? Could he fit them together? For some reason, Steven remained unsure. "But how did Cham know so much more about the afterlife than I did? He was the one that explained things to me. He knew more than I did. That doesn't make sense."

Vic offered an honest answer. "It might seem like Cham knew things you didn't, but only because you made it that way. When your soul is freed, your perception to all things opens up. You had the answers before you, but it was easier for you to place those answers in Cham. You asked questions, Cham answered them for you. It made more sense that way for you."

"Why?"

"Simple. You created Cham to be more than just a vessel for your doubts and fears. When you died, you weren't sure where to go. You weren't ready to be with God, that's why you made the door that blocked your way to Him. At that point, you still needed direction and that's when Cham arrived. You made him out to be some kind of guide. But you did more than that. In order for you to give substance to your doubts, you placed them right along side everything your spiritual perception told you about the afterlife. Cham didn't know more than you did. You just surrendered that knowledge to him to give that much more substance to your fears. You didn't want to argue with yourself, so you made Cham. It's hard to ignore your doubts when they come from someone that seems to know what's going on around you. You made your struggle as difficult as possible."

Thoughts of Cham now ran slightly clearer in Steven's mind. He thought back to those first moments in the afterlife. "Cham said he wasn't a guardian angel and that he had nothing to do with my life on earth. That wasn't quite true, either. Cham was inside of me all the time, from the very beginning."

This much was now very obvious to Steven. He pondered Cham's first appearance, put it in perspective against a new consideration. Steven had accepted death almost immediately. It was not the same with God. He held off on that acceptance.

That's when he gave Chamuel substance and form, and that's when Steven's true test began.

"Cham was nothing more than me deciding if I should deny God," Steven admitted. "He was the manifestation of my own doubts and my disbeliefs. Just like I created and then shut the door on God, I created someone that would be a voice for advocating a separation from God."

Vic put his hand on his grandson's shoulder. "Just about everyone that ends up on earth has doubts, but you decided to rise above them. I'm proud of you for that. The name Chamuel was actually the name for an Archangel. The name stands for 'He who seeks God', and that means something. You gave him that name. Even when your doubts did manifest themselves, you still wanted to get through them. You were still seeking God, not seeking to deny Him. You just had to face your own reservations, and in the end, you did."

"So you saw all that? You could see me speaking with Cham?"

"Yes, I could. As I said, I wasn't sure you were going to get past that. It's not like it's written in stone, you know. You really did have to make up your own mind. That's the way it works, that's the way it always works."

"I guess I know that now, too." Steven admitted and he realized the moment he threw open that door, he also cast aside his own doubts about life and where God should be in his. The puzzle, however, was still not complete.

"Where was I really?" Steven asked. "For some reason, I can't figure that out. I know I was dead. I also know I wasn't in heaven, but it was like heaven. I could do anything I wanted. I just had to do it without God. I was somehow trapped in between."

"You've got it figured out perfectly. You were at the doorway to heaven, but you weren't ready to come inside. On earth, some might call it purgatory."

This is what Steven could not understand. "But God

wouldn't send me to purgatory. He's here now and I know that. I know that as sure as I know I'm here talking to you."

"That's very true, but God won't make your decisions for you, either. That's why it's not quite clear to you yet. You know God would never do you harm, but He won't stop you from harming yourself if that's what you're intent on doing."

A piece came a bit clearer and Steven put it into words. "I put myself in that situation, didn't I? I didn't come all the way across. I kept the door shut and then I had Cham show up to try and convince me to stay out. I did it all to myself."

"Yes, you did, and you were not easy on yourself. The truth is that God doesn't send us to hell and God doesn't make us wait in purgatory. He would never do that. We choose to go to hell and we create our own purgatory. Again, that's the way it has to work, otherwise it really wouldn't mean anything to be here now."

Steven nodded.

"Listen," Vic stated with an edge of excitement cutting his words, "there's a great many people here that are looking forward to seeing you, friends and relatives you never knew you had, but there's something you and I have to do first. We're both not quite done yet and that's another reason why you still have a question or two. I'm sorry about that, but there's no way around it."

"We have to go back to earth, don't we?" Steven asked.

"Yes, we both have unfinished business," Vic answered just as the mountains in the distance and the trees nearby faded away into a white mist. Barely a moment in heaven, and for some reason, Steven had to return to earth once more.

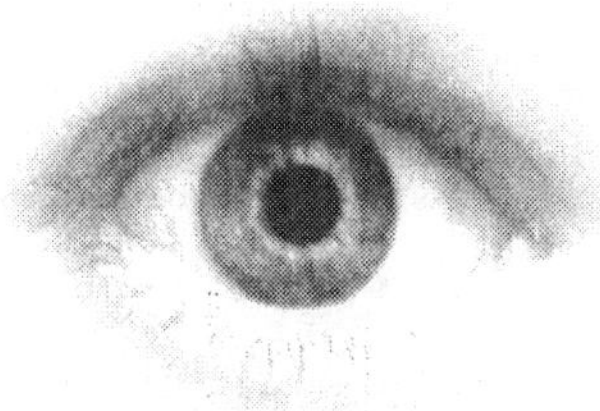

TRUST

Steven and Vic arrived at a place Steven did not immediately recognize. He stood upon a vast and elevated plateau that overlooked a series of hilltops which stretched out into the horizon. The bases of the hills formed several narrow valleys and most of the land directly below was covered in tall grass with only a few trees dotting the landscape.

Far in the distance, he recognized a small town. Upon further inspection, he believed, in fact, it was the town close to where he used to live. He scanned the roads and they followed a pattern that matched his memory. As more areas became familiar, he began to find landmarks that supported his conclusion. He pinpointed the main street, the church steeple, as well as the tallest structures of the community.

Upon establishing his bearings, he noted the location of several parks, schools, shopping centers, and finally the river. With these points of reference firmly in mind, he looked for even more personal points of interest.

He could not see his house from where he stood. Of course, it was no longer there, but he couldn't even locate the slab foundation. He could only roughly estimate the location. Still, he could see the road that led from the river to his front yard and he followed it to the places he used to go when he once lived in this place.

While he definitely knew the area in the distance, the same could not be said for the ground he stood upon at that moment. He knew he was somewhat close to his previous home, but this particular stretch of earth was not a place he had ever visited before. It was higher ground and much more desolate. He noted a few dirt paths, but no paved roads and no indication of any significant use.

Giving the immediate area a closer inspection, he scanned his surroundings attempting to find something even vaguely familiar. A much more wooded area stood off to his right, and within those trees, he noticed a small stream that weaved its way through the light forest. The stream ran toward him as it broke from the trees and hit a clearing with a steep decline. The downward current reached such speed that it was almost a free flowing water fall. The water, however, never actually separated from the ground. It simply dashed downward to one of the small valleys below and disappeared out of sight.

Just beyond this stream and passed a small embankment, Steven finally saw the lake. He wondered how he missed it until this point, for it covered a huge portion of the plateau. If anything, it overwhelmed the entire landscape and made the stream appear like a small trickle of water in comparison.

Despite its size, this body of water just did not appear natural to Steven. Its borders and embankments looked as if they were constructed by man and not by nature. It also seemed out of place on this plateau. He imagined it would have been much more useful down in the foothills. Here, it was out of reach to just about everyone. Steven wondered if it was maybe some kind of backup reservoir.

With that thought in mind, Steven wondered if maybe the town was currently suffering from some drought, for the lake appeared as if it was only half-full. His gaze ran along the dry cracked mud near the water's edge and around the rim until he caught sight of the large gap in the far embankment which separated the lake from the hillside below it. At that moment, he knew.

In his mind, he followed a path down the hillside and through the narrow valleys below. He imagined a large flow of water racing downward and where it would go. He scanned a path right to the river's edge and then his sight followed the river itself from that point until its first major bend. Once more he found the lonely road that led to where his house used to sit.

"That's what caused the flood," Steven said more to himself but loud enough for Vic to hear. "The embankment gave way and the water rushed down the hills until it hit the river. All that water broke over the river bank and into that flood plain right there, but there was too much water and it went down the road right into my house. That's how I died."

"You're right on that," Vic acknowledged. "That's exactly what happened."

"But that's not why we're here, is it."

"It's part of why we're here, but you're right again, it's not the real reason. We're here to find someone. There's someone you need to talk to."

"Who?"

"The person who built this reservoir. He's still here."

"He's dead, isn't he?" Steven asked, but for some reason, he already knew it was true.

"Yes."

"And he hasn't accepted his death. That's why he's still here."

"Let's just go find him."

Flying high in the air, Vic and Steven commanded a view of the entire lake. They spotted the form of a young man sitting between the edge of the water and the trees where the stream ran. Vic and Steven floated down to this form with deliberate care.

At first, the man seemed not to notice. He simply stared off into the distance beyond the hills.

Vic turned to Steven. "Talk to him, learn his story. It's important."

Steven found no reason to argue the claim. If anything, he felt compelled to reach out to the apparition before him. He felt as if a link existed, though he could not explain why.

"Hello," Steven called for the young man's attention. "Are you alright?"

"No. It didn't work."

This response just raised more questions.

"What didn't work?" Steven asked.

"My plan. It didn't work."

"What was your plan?"

The young man appeared to be speaking more to himself as opposed to answering any direct questions. "I don't know, maybe I was meant to fail from the very beginning. It was all my fault. Why should I be surprised it didn't work? It was a bad plan anyway. I'm actually surprised anyone believed me at all in the first place, but I had designed power plants before, that's why they trusted me. I made them trust me, but I didn't have a choice. I needed their money."

The man then shook his head and looked out over the large body of water.

"What's your name?" Steven asked.

"Raymond."

"Raymond, what does a power plant have to do with money and why you're here?"

Raymond finally looked up at Steven. Sorrow filled his face, a deep painful sadness that had a life of its own. It seemed as if Raymond recognized Steven, though Steven did not share the feeling. This was a total stranger before him.

As if looking into Steven's face for too long caused him pain, Raymond removed his glance and staggered to his feet. He walked to the edge of the lake as he continued his story.

"I convinced them. I can't believe I was able to do that. Anyone that would look around would know it wasn't going to work. Too many obstacles. The ground wasn't right. There would never be sufficient pressure. Eventually you could build the powerhouse, but you'd never generate enough electricity to offset the cost. But I told them it would all work out. I designed enough of them that maybe they just wanted to believe me, believe that I could make them even more money. It was easy to convince them then. I didn't like it, but I had to. It's not like the worst sin I ever committed."

"You were going to build a power plant here?"

"No, it would never have gone that far. I showed them the problems after the reservoir was built. I wasn't going to take all their money, but I had to get them to go along to get things started."

Steven took a deep long look into the man before him. He knew the man was suffering from some past event, some distant recollection of a perceived failing. He also knew there was a reason he was here now. Steven looked deeper into Raymond, but not with his eyes. Instead, Steven viewed the tormented apparition with the perception of one soul to another. In that moment, Raymond's death became visible.

It was almost like stepping into someone else's memory. Steven could see Raymond's thoughts right before him like a large moving picture projected into blank space, and then suddenly, Steven became a part of that very scene. It was no longer simply a projection of thought, it was much more encompassing. Steven felt as if he actually existed in that moment in time and that he could relive it at will.

It appeared to Steven as if he now stood in the middle of a small and dreary office. He noticed old equipment like a mechanical typewriter and a slide rule sitting on a heavy wooden desk. Raymond, looking somewhat older, sat behind that desk. He looked tired and worn.

Two angry men that Steven did not recognize were already

in the office standing in front of Raymond's desk. The man that stood closest to Raymond towered over him. His emotions ran unchecked and he appeared ready to smash his fist through a wall. The second man's anger was much more controlled, and in this, Steven actually smelled danger.

While the two strangers clearly confronted Raymond with seething animosity, they paid no mind to Steven's appearance. Of course they couldn't see him, for they were only the vacant images of Raymond's recollection, and Steven was nothing more than an invisible and silent observer of a painful yet significant memory.

"What are you telling us?" The larger of the two men asked Raymond. "You're saying we have to stop?"

"It's the smartest decision at this point," Raymond answered with true regret in his voice. "It's not going to work. The reservoir just won't hold as much water that's necessary to keep the turbines moving consistently for any period of time. If we open the penstock, the reservoir will drain completely in a month, maybe two. It won't refill fast enough."

"I thought you said you could divert all the surrounding streams to take care of that."

"That's the problem. I thought there was enough water, but I've been studying it for the last few months while we were digging out the embankments. The streams don't have sufficient water flow. More water will drain out than what will come in."

"You showed us those streams, there was plenty of water!" the larger man shouted as he became more agitated by the second.

"There was more snow melt than normal when we first measured the output. It was an irregularity. That kind of flow is only going to occur for a couple of months during the spring and only after winters of very heavy snowfalls. You wouldn't be able to count on it for continuous operation."

"How could you have made that kind of mistake? You were

this genius with water that knew how to design these things! You're supposed to be an expert?"

Raymond looked down at the surface of his desk. "I don't know how I missed it, but you have to face facts now. The reservoir would be an exceptional mill pond to run a few factories, but it can't possibly generate the kind of electricity that would justify building the power station. If you go forward with further construction, you'll never get that money back."

"What about the money for the surveys, architects, and engineering designs? What about all the damn money for creating that reservoir?! How are we going to get that back?"

"Would you prefer to lose more?" Raymond asked without looking up. "Because that's what will happen if you keep going forward."

"So that's it? You just tell us it isn't going to work out and you think we just shrug our shoulders and leave?"

Raymond finally forced himself to lift his head and face his questioners. "I'm trying to give you the best advice I can."

At this point the smaller man entered the conversation. "We spent a great deal of money on you. You were the expert. You told us this spot would work, now you're telling us differently. I will not simply accept this loss. There will be repercussions. I will sue you for everything you have."

"I have nothing," Raymond said. "I invested everything I had right along with you. All the fees you paid me, every penny I had went into this project. I have nothing left for you to take from me."

"What are you talking about? You're investment was minimal at best. The fees we paid you were four times what you invested."

"My money went to a project that would benefit from the initial construction, but it didn't work out as planned. It's gone. I have nothing left. You can look through my accounts. You'll see it's all gone."

"And you think by telling me this, that's going to satisfy me?"

"No, I think by telling you this I will be saving you future losses. I wish I could do something about the past, but I can't. That's been the story of my life."

"I see," the smaller man acknowledged as he turned about and never looked back. Before he left the room, he gave a final order to his partner. "Kill him and sink his body in the middle of that reservoir. Then that will be the story of his death."

The command shocked Raymond into a frozen stupor. He sat motionless at his desk watching the smaller man's back trail through the doorway and out of sight.

The larger man, however, moved with speed and skill. In an instant, the big man was around the desk and directly behind Raymond. He grabbed Raymond's chin with one large, fleshy palm as he wrapped his other arm around Raymond's throat to grab the back of his shoulder. With a powerful and deadly quick twist, the large man snapped the neck of his intended victim. He then plucked Raymond's lifeless body from the chair and threw it over his shoulder.

The office melted from Steven's view as darkness fell over the scene. It was the darkness of an overcast night sky reflecting off the still surface of a manmade lake. Steven was now back at the reservoir and it looked much the same. The large man was present once more, except this time he was in a small row boat with a large bundle that looked like an oversized sack of potatoes. Steven understood that this was certainly Raymond's corpse, and as directed, the beefy killer took hold of the weighted-down body and threw it into the center of the lake.

The splash of water threw a mist in the air that grew into an all encompassing fog. Everywhere Steven looked, he saw a hazy vapor that eventually turned everything blank white.

As if someone clapped his hands, Steven was brought back to the edge of the lake by a loud crack. He had witnessed Raymond's final moments in life, and he believed he understood.

"So you had this reservoir built," Steven said to the apparition. "You swindled some people into believing they could build a hydroelectric power plant, but you just took their money instead. They killed you and dumped you here for what you did."

Raymond would not acknowledge anything Steven said at this point. He simply stared vacantly out over the water toward the hills.

Steven felt no anger, but he followed the apparent connection that brought him here.

"This lake was abandoned after that. It served no purpose. Eventually, one of the embankments gave way and it caused a flood, the flood that destroyed my house. I died in that flood."

"I'm sorry," Raymond stated without turning about.

Steven still felt no animosity toward this man. If anything, he felt pity for a lost soul that remained caught at this lakeside for untold years.

"It's okay, I don't blame you."

"No, I'm sorry!"

Steven shook his head. "You don't have to be. You didn't mean to cause that flood. It just happened. I don't know why you tricked those men, but you never intended to hurt me. And it looks like you already paid way too much for what you did."

"I don't care about those men and their money."

"Look, if you want me to forgive you, it's done. I don't hold anything against you."

"No!" Raymond shouted and he turned about revealing an expression of frustration and pain. There was anger there, too.

Steven almost stepped back in surprise. "I don't know what you want from me."

At this point, Vic stepped between them, but turned his focus solely on Steven. "He's not saying he's sorry for what he did to you. He doesn't even think you're dead. He thinks you're just as alive as he is. He's saying he's sorry for something else."

"I don't understand," Steven admitted.

"Not yet, but you will. Think about what he's saying. There

are still questions you have to ask. You don't know the whole story yet. Fill in the blanks and you will get your answer."

Steven acknowledged he did not truly know what was going on anymore. He thought he was here to better understand his own death, to know why the flood occurred, and that was certainly part of it. There was, however, much more to be considered beyond the flood, more to Raymond's agony. He could not imagine what part he had to play, but there was something here Steven needed to do, a path he needed to follow, both for his benefit and Raymond's. As he contemplated the story he had seen, one question came clear into his mind.

"Why did you really want to build this reservoir?"

"It was desperation," Raymond responded—still angry, still frustrated.

"What were you desperate about? Did you need money?"

"I only needed money to get the reservoir built."

Steven felt they were about to travel in a never ending circle, and he couldn't allow that. In some way, he knew he needed to get the young man to admit the truth of his desires.

"But why?" Steven pressed. "You knew all along the reservoir couldn't be used for a power plant. I understand that, so why did you want it built?"

"I thought it might lower the river enough."

"Lower the river?"

Raymond's frustration appeared to grow, even as his anger turned more into despair.

"It was a desperate gamble. I admit it. No one was going to let me dam up the river, that's what I wanted to do, but there was no way to do it effectively. The moment I started building a dam, they would have stopped me. But if I could convince them a hydroelectric plant could be built, I could have succeeded, but there were too many problems. The elevations were all wrong. Everything was denied."

"But it wasn't denied," Steven countered. He struggled to follow Raymond's explanation, but something was still missing.

"The reservoir was built. It's here right now. Look around. And those two men, they were ready to build the plant. What do you mean it was denied?"

"The dam was denied," Raymond shot back. "That's what I really wanted, but I didn't have a choice. The river was too important for people. It was then I got the idea to build up here, to cutoff some of the river's source. There were always people with money that wanted to make more. If I could convince them to invest in a reservoir up here, I could get it done with minimal objections. No one knew what I had in mind for the river."

"What does this lake have to do with the river?"

"This is all runoff. We diverted streams and creeks to the north to fill it up, waterways that would normally feed the river. It would also temporarily stop the snowmelt runoff from the higher grounds. I thought it would be enough to drop the river level by a couple of feet and that might be enough."

"Enough for what?

"Enough to find her!"

"Find who?"

"My mother. She drowned in that river."

This revelation hit Steven hard. Finally, he began to understand. "She drowned a long time ago, didn't she?"

Raymond said nothing.

"Did you push your mother off of a riverboat?"

"NO! I didn't push her. It was tag."

"It was what?"

"I wanted to play tag. She wasn't feeling good. She said the smell made her sick. She went to the front of the boat to get away from it. I felt bad for her. We always played tag and that made her happy. I snuck up on her and tagged her in the back."

"So it was an accident."

"I didn't mean for her to fall off. I thought she was trying to turn around and tag me back like she always does, but then before I knew it, she was gone, so I ran and hid."

"You were afraid you were going to get in trouble, weren't you?"

"I didn't mean to push her! It was just a game! We were supposed to have fun. I was laughing when she fell."

Steven remembered Laura's death, the death he had experienced in the river, the death that Laura herself could not accept. He recalled the face of the smiling boy. He knew that boy was Raymond.

"That's why the boat didn't stop," Steven muttered. "No one knew she fell off the boat but you. And you ran and hid."

Despite how it sounded, the words were not accusatory in nature. They were the simple collection of fact. Through Laura's eyes, he saw the riverboat sail away. She did not know why it didn't stop for her, but now he did.

"I eventually told," Raymond revealed through a gasp, "but it was too late. We were too far down the river to turn back, and I wasn't sure exactly where it happened. We never saw her again. I knew she drowned, she had to. She would have found us if she swam to shore. I knew she was in the river, but I just couldn't find her. That's why I wanted to lower the level of the river. Just a few feet might have been enough to find her."

More of the puzzle came into focus for Steven. "So that's why you built the reservoir."

"It did work for a while, at least a little bit. The river level did drop and I rented a boat and paid for other people to help me search. That's what I did with all the money. I didn't take any for myself, but nobody found anything because I couldn't remember exactly where she fell. We didn't have much time, only a few days. Then the river went right back to its normal level. If I could have built the dam, I would have found her."

"Why are you here, Raymond?" Steven demanded. "Why here and not the river? If you still wanted to find your mother, you should be looking at the river."

"Because I don't know where in the river to look! This was my last hope. Building this reservoir was my last chance. There was nothing left to do when I couldn't find her, no where else to go. I thought maybe if she knew I built this to find her, maybe if she knew how far I went, maybe she would forgive me."

In that instant, Steven felt a surge of hope beyond his understanding of the moment. This was more than a terrible accident and two lost souls that could not find each other or their way into the next life. He wasn't sure why, but somehow Steven knew that this was a chance afforded to him to find an answer, an answer to his own search for the truth.

"Raymond, if you trust me, I can help you. You'll have to follow me. You'll have to leave this place and go down to the river. I can take you to her. I know where your mother is."

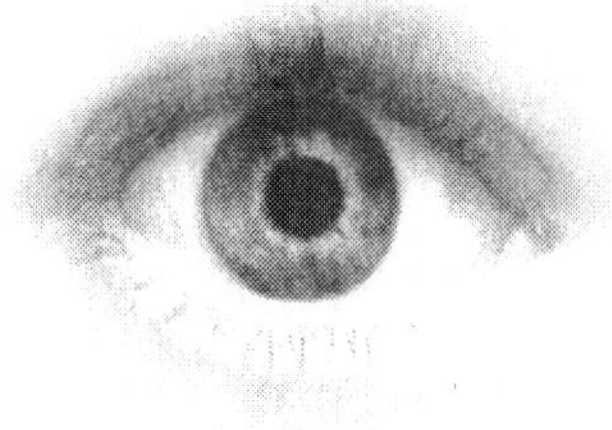

LIBERATION

"Where is she?"

"You were right, she drowned in the river."

Raymond went quiet, as if to internalize this turn of events based on his own circumstances. News such as this has no true victory. While there is certain closure in removing the unknowns, there is misery in substance. He seemed torn at first, perhaps unwilling to accept this as the final verdict. If it was true, he would know now that she had not simply abandoned them, or that she had not spent months or years desperately seeking her son, just as he suffered over seeming ages in seeking her. But of course, it also meant he would have to accept the staggering reality that his actions, despite his innocent intentions, still caused his mother's death.

As that realization took hold, any solace in the thought of finally determining what ultimately happened to his mother disintegrated in a furious burst of sorrow.

Raymond dropped his face into his hands and began to weep.

Steven stood silent, patiently waiting for the apparition to release at least a fraction of his sorrow. There was little else he could do.

Eventually, Raymond found his voice once more. "How did you find her?"

In responding, Steven finally focused on far more than the link between two lost souls, mother and son. He thought of his own connection, his part in this complex series of events. This was not just about the flood that took his life. He had found Laura in the middle of the river for a reason, and he was brought here to meet with Raymond to do something important. It just wasn't quite clear to him yet, but his focus was sharpening and the puzzle pieces arranged themselves before him in orderly fashion. He just needed to press them together.

"I'm not sure," Steven admitted. "I just stumbled on her. Actually, now that I think about it, I don't think stumbling had anything to do with it. I believe I was meant to find her."

"What are you talking about?" Raymond demanded, his own despair spurring both anger and uncertainty.

Steven thought deeply now of his involvement. Cham had brought him to the river, but Cham was really only a part of himself. He didn't know for sure he would find anything there, but something within him must have guided him to that spot, guided him to Laura. And now, here he was with Laura's son.

Steven turned to Vic, for it was Vic that brought him to this lake. "Why did you bring me here?"

Vic, however, would not elaborate, not yet anyway.

"We'll get into that when it's time. Right now you need to focus on Raymond. It's important. You know that."

Steven could not argue that point. He was playing a role in a larger matter, and his questions would wait.

"Tell him how you found his mother," Vic urged.

"For some reason, I went looking down the river," Steven said as he turned back to Raymond. "There was something I needed to see, something that would help me understand things. I don't know quite how to explain it, but I was basically following my own doubts. That might not make sense to you, but it's starting to get clearer to me. Anyway, I followed the river downstream from a place very near here, a place where I used to live. While I was following the river, I noticed something odd in the middle of the water. I went to investigate and I saw her."

"So you found the body?"

Steven did not respond directly to this question. He knew Raymond had not accepted his own death. Raymond believed he was still alive and hoping to find his mother's corpse. If Steven simply stated he saw a lost spirit, Raymond might stop listening all together. That would not do, and so Steven remained somewhat evasive in his answer.

"Well, I wasn't sure what I found at first. She had been there a long time, you understand. But I'm sure it's your mother. Her name was Laura, wasn't it?"

Raymond didn't even ask how Steven could possibly learn this from a corpse. "Yes, it was. Then you did find her. She was in the river . . . I knew she never got out. I knew it!"

At this point, Steven saw clearly both the hope and despair in Raymond's spirit. The two opposing emotions tore at the apparition and they played a critical role in Raymond's inability to leave this place. Steven was certain that Raymond remained at this lake because it was his last hope in finding his mother, but it was also a testament to an understanding that his mother had drowned by his hand. Now, Steven brought information to Raymond that would verify that belief. Steven knew that if he didn't act swiftly, he might ultimately fail in what he believed he had to do.

"I don't think it's a good idea for you to simply take my word for it." Steven stated. "You've been looking and waiting a long time. You need to be absolutely sure. For you to really believe, I think you have to see for yourself. Don't you agree?"

Raymond nodded furiously. "Yes, I need to see. I need to be sure. I have to be absolutely sure."

"Nothing I can say at this point can do that for you, but if you follow me, I'll show you what I found. You can make up your own mind after that. If you think I'm wrong, you can come back here and I won't bother you again."

At this request, Raymond hesitated.

"I have to leave here?"

"I can't bring her to you," Steven said and he knew that to be the God's honest truth. "You have to come to her. That's the way it has to be."

Once more Raymond broke down into sobs. "I know . . . I know . . . it's my fault, so I have to go. I have to find her, but. . . ." His voice trailed off into a fit of tears.

"But what?" Steven questioned.

"I don't know if I can leave here!"

"I think you can," Steven said boldly. "If you want to see her bad enough, then it doesn't matter what happened here, does it?"

"You're right!" Raymond said almost defiantly. "They can't keep me here. They can't keep me from her."

Steven knew that Raymond was referring to the two men that were responsible for Raymond's death, the ones that made sure this reservoir was his last resting place. He would not, however, speak of the two, for that would make Raymond face certain truths about his own end, and Steven didn't want that to happen just yet.

"No one can keep you from her if you really want to see her," Steven stepped closer to Raymond hoping to encourage the young man to follow. "It won't take long. We can be there before night falls. I'm sure of it. If you give me the chance, I can help you find her. How long have you been waiting for this?"

"A long time," Raymond admitted.

"Long enough to take a chance on following me and allowing your search to be over by tonight?"

"Yes."

Steven turned and looked to the horizon. He could see the river. They could fly there in no time, but he knew Raymond had not accepted his own death. Raymond believed he was still constrained in a mortal body. They would have to walk.

"We can make it down the side of this hill and then follow the lower grounds to the river." Steven turned to Vic. "Are you alright with all this?"

Vic gave Raymond a long look before responding to Steven's question. "You're doing fine. Just keep following your instincts on this. Don't worry about me."

Steven returned his attention to Raymond. "It's not a long walk. We can make it. Are you willing to give it a try?"

"Yes," Raymond responded through a mumble.

Steven took the lead, following the edge of the reservoir to the breach that caused the flood which took his life. Following the same path down the hillside and toward the river would be the shortest route.

Raymond followed silently and obediently until he came to the point of the break in the bank. At the edge of the hillside, he stopped completely. He looked down toward the river only for a moment, and then he turned about and stared out into the water, stared at the exact point where the large man had dumped his body.

"You can come back here, if you have to," Steven prodded, "but your mother's not here." Steven waited for Raymond to look back over his shoulder. When he did, Steven pointed toward the river. "She's down there. That's where you have to go now."

But Raymond would not move.

Steven forced the issue. "You built this to find her, that's what you said. If this place means something to you, then it has a purpose. What good is a purpose if you don't follow through with it? If you stay here, then this place really is meaningless, isn't it?"

Raymond bowed his head. "Yes." He turned his back on the lake and followed Steven down the hill.

It was not a difficult journey. None of them were physical

beings struggling with exhaustion or physical limitations over harsh terrain. They simply maintained the appearance of walking down steep slopes and through thick brush as they made their way to the river's edge.

Once there, Steven shot a smile over to Raymond. "See, we're here. No problems. It won't be long now. It's not far from here at all."

The three spirits continued to hike downstream and, as the sun fell low on the horizon, the surface of the river sparkled except where the shadows of the trees stretched over the water. The current ran steady, giving the reflected sunlight a movement all its own.

Surprisingly, they passed no one save a lone fisherman. Knee-deep in the water with a line cast across to the opposite side of the river, he paid mind only to the shadows of fish he swore he saw. If somehow he might have sensed the presence of three ghosts somberly shambling past him, he would have dismissed them as the whispers of long past fishermen seeking refuge in the sanctity of the river. He would have understood this, for he would have expected no different of himself.

With the shadows growing darker and a few fireflies adorning the tall weeds, turning them into summertime Christmas trees, Steven knew they were approaching the spot where he encountered his first lost soul. He gazed a bit further downstream and into the center of the river. He found her just as he left her, in the middle of the water waiting for someone to return, waiting for her son.

The angled rays of the setting sun lit up the smoky gray haze of her essence giving it a purple hue like a cloud drifting across a powerful sunset. Steven wondered how Raymond would react in seeing this misty apparition of his mother.

"Raymond," Steven called for the young man's attention. "We're very close now. What you see might upset you, but I believe with all my soul you need to see this. Whatever happens, understand that at some point you have to forgive yourself for what was a total accident."

"What are you saying?" Raymond asked with a stunned expression crossing his glimmering face that was becoming translucent in the fading sunlight.

"You just need to keep an open mind, that's all," Steven responded at a loss for further explanation. "Give me a moment, so I can check on your mother. Then I'll bring you to her."

It was Steven's intention to go out alone to the center of the river and at least prepare Laura for their arrival. He never got the chance.

Out in the water, the gray mist swirled. It grew and took shape. The clear definition of a head and shoulders of a woman rose up from the river and it turned to the three with a wide-eyed look of wonder.

She glided toward them slowly, and as she did, more of her body rose out of the water and into sight. She reached the shores apparently soaking wet, but not a drop of water fell from her figure to the ground. She looked directly at Raymond and she knew, she knew her son had returned for her.

"Raymond?"

"Mom?"

The two embraced, but only for a moment. Laura released her hold and stepped back from her son. She could not fight the question that burned in her mind since the moment of her death. It dropped from her essence like a heavy chain.

"Why did you push me?" she cried.

Her retreat and her question did not surprise her son. He expected it. It was part of the guilt that weighed him down through both life and death. He deserved no less.

"I didn't mean to," Raymond pleaded.

"You were smiling!" Laura stated with an accusing stare.

"It was an accident."

"You didn't come get me . . . the boat kept going. . . ."

"I was afraid. I didn't tell anyone what happened."

"Why were you smiling?!"

"It was supposed to be a game!" Raymond shouted back.

"A game?"

"Tag. Remember how we played tag?"

"You were playing?"

"I tagged you, that was all. I didn't want you to fall."

And with that, Laura finally understood. She understood everything. She knew it was truly an accident. She knew her son did not mean to push her over. She knew he was smiling because he thought it was just a game. She also knew she had died.

Comprehension came in one single wave—her rejection of death, the rejection of God—and she renounced both. The full measure of her past and future returned to her. Laura remembered everything and accepted everything. She also reclaimed her faith in God and wanted nothing more than to be with Him. This is where she differed from Steven.

Steven accepted his death immediately, but not God. Laura took untold decades to accept her death, but when she did, she would not deny God for even an instant, for she understood what this moment truly meant.

Her form took on even greater detail and she smiled gratefully as she turned not to her son, but toward Steven.

"You brought him to me. You found us both. Thank you."

"I don't think we're done yet," Steven admitted.

Looking back at Raymond, Laura understood his ordeal as well. "Oh Raymond, you can't do this to yourself." Laura could almost see the very misery she had been through etched in Raymond's face. It would have torn her soul into pieces, but something buffered the pain. She did not want him to go through the same agony, but she could not make the choice for him.

"He tried very hard to find you," Steven explained. "He was murdered in the process."

It didn't hurt to hear that her son was murdered, not like it would have hurt if she had still been alive on earth. The pain of that world had finally been removed from her. While freed from her own suffering, she made the attempt to save Raymond from his self-induced punishment. "No, Raymond, no. You can't do this to yourself."

Raymond's guilt remained. He might have explained himself to his mother, but nothing said so far released him from his own declaration of fault. He had killed his mother, that he knew, and yet there was now talk of something he could not fathom. He had deceived others in hopes of finding his mother's body, but he could recall no murder. As he looked into his mother's face, he saw concern, even pity for his own situation. He did not want any of this.

"What are you two talking about? What do you think I'm doing to myself? What do you mean I was murdered?"

"I did drown," Laura declared without hesitation. "I did. I didn't want to believe it, either. I understand what you're doing to yourself, but you can't do it anymore. Now you have to see, just like I can see."

"I know you drowned. I pushed you. It was my fault."

"No, it was an accident, but that's not what I'm talking about. You can't go on punishing yourself. Think about what's going on here."

"I know what's going on here! I found you. I finally found you! And you're. . . ."

He did not complete his statement, and so Laura did so for him.

"Dead."

A puzzled expression turned quickly to pure confusion and then panic.

"How can you be standing here before me if you're dead?"

"Raymond," Laura said with a newfound strength in her voice. "Do you know why I'm still here? I couldn't believe that I had died the way I did. I didn't *want* to believe it. I stayed here because it was easier for me to question everything than to accept the truth. That's what you're doing now."

"The only thing I questioned was what happened to you!"

Raymond stated as if he was on trial, not for drowning his mother, but for some mysterious deed that was now somehow hidden from him.

"And what happened to you?" Laura demanded.

"I don't know. People wouldn't help me find you. They tried to stop me. I ran out of ideas. I didn't know what else to do, so I just stayed up at the water, stayed at the last thing I tried, my last failure."

"And you've just been staying there ever since? Just like I stayed in this river?"

"Well, yes . . . and no. You drowned. I didn't drown."

"But you're still in the water, aren't you?"

Raymond was becoming angry. "I did what I had to do. Now I don't know what's going on anymore."

Steven intervened. "All you wanted to do was find your mother. That's all. You've done that. You didn't fail. You've found her and you released her from the river. What do you have left to do?"

Raymond began to visibly shake. "I don't know, but something seems wrong about this. It doesn't make any sense. So I found her? So what? It doesn't change things."

"It does for her."

"He's right," Laura agreed. "I can leave now. You can come with me."

"No, I can't. I have to get back to the . . . I have to go back. Something's not right."

He would say nothing further. He might have found his mother, but he had not yet found the full truth. Raymond ran back upstream without looking back.

Steven knew where he was going—back to the reservoir. As he watched Raymond dash beyond the trees, he didn't feel sadness or frustration, and it wasn't quite confusion. There wasn't even a sense of failure in this turn of events. He knew Raymond did not accept death, and was thus linking himself to this existence for a time to come, but in looking at Laura, he knew it didn't have to be that way forever.

Still, he felt he owed Laura an apology. "I'm sorry. I thought I could help him."

Laura's spirit glistened in the dying sunlight. She no longer appeared soaking wet, only shining with joy. "You did, in a way." Laura knew that at least part of Raymond's path was now clear. He knew the truth, and that was the first step. Hopefully, the next steps would not be as hard, nor take as long. "You helped both of us. You brought him to me which was what he wanted. Now, he has to figure out what that means to him. You've done all that you could possibly do for him."

While he himself did not feel sadness in Raymond's departure, Steven questioned Laura's abrupt change. "He's your son. Don't you feel bad for him?"

Laura looked out toward the hills in the direction Raymond departed, and it almost seemed she could still see him. "I can't explain it. I don't want him to suffer in any way. And for him to suffer means I should suffer, but I'm beyond that now. I understand what he's going through. I know what he's thinking, and in a way, so do you." She stopped there, but only for a moment. "Then again, maybe you don't see it all yet. You're almost there, you're so close. What you have left is so small, but you have to let it all go."

Steven heard these words and they forced him to open up to one last truth. There was indeed one last issue for him to sort through. He could not grasp it completely yet. It almost seemed to buzz about his mind like a gnat around his face on a humid day.

"I know there's something else," Steven admitted, "but it's still a bit fuzzy."

"I can see that," Laura sounded almost surprised. "But you've already made your decision, you just don't want to accept it. God is with you now. I can see that, too. Everything is so clear to me. It came in like a wave. Everything I questioned, everything I didn't understand. It all makes sense. Even Raymond. Maybe because I've been dead longer than you, I can really understand things now. You were guided to me."

"By Cham," Steven stated out loud, but he knew it was not Cham, because Cham was just a part of himself. Laura, however, knew the real truth.

"No, by God. You did have a purpose, don't ever doubt that. The reservoir, the flood, the river, your house—all of it lined up to help me. Even when you first came across me, you knew you needed to help me. All of that just to save me from myself."

She looked off into the distance again. "Maybe that's why I'm not worried about Raymond. He's closer to finding himself, closer than I ever was. I know despite what he's going through, it's not over for him. You helped me. Someone will help him, or he'll help himself. He has to figure it out for himself anyway, just like I did. Just like you will. Don't feel bad. Even if we give up on God, He never gives up on us. That's why you're here. I understand that now, and so should you."

She said nothing more, she simply faded out of sight.

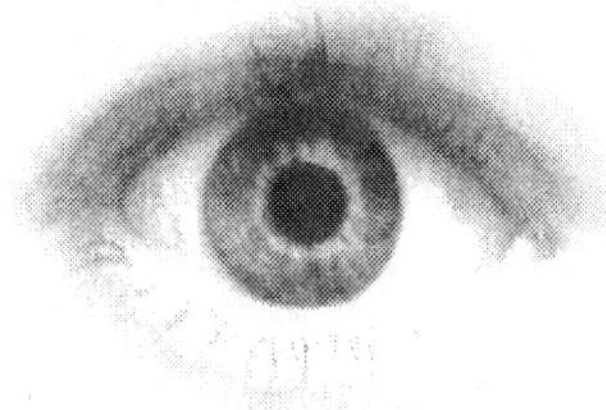

COMPREHENSION

She's right, you know." Vic declared as it was now just him and Steven alone by the edge of the river.

"I know," Steven replied. "I was here for a reason. My doubts created Cham, and Cham brought me to Laura. Now Laura's free. Even in my doubts, I ended up helping someone else. That's not just a coincidence. That's the hand of God reaching out to us, reaching out to us all."

"So, you see that now. It's getting clearer to you. That means we really are almost done here."

"I know that, too," Steven replied. "Almost everything is starting to come together. There's one last issue, but it's not about Raymond anymore. Laura was right about that as well. He has to figure it out on his own. There's nothing more I can do for him. There's only one question left to answer, and that's my issue, not his."

"Which is?"

Steven hesitated, as if he did not want to speak of the topic, but the moments for silence had past. It was time to face his last question regarding life and death. "The spider. When I was with

Cham, when he still tried to convince me to stay away from God, why did I focus on the spider?"

"I guess that is the last thing for you to figure out. It's not an easy one, I'll grant you, but you need to face it. Maybe you need to look at the bigger picture for that one."

"In all honesty, it's hard for me not to look at the big picture any more. None of this was just about me. I died because a wall burst for a reservoir that was built years ago to find a drowned mother. I ended up finding that woman and I know it wasn't just an accident. I don't want it to sound like I feel used. If anything, I'm grateful, grateful that even though I couldn't bring myself to be with God the moment I died, God found a way to use me to help someone else. That's a pretty potent feeling. I know I mattered, even while I was fighting my own uncertainties, I was important."

"But you wonder why the spider wasn't important, or why there are so many insignificant creatures that have to suffer in this world. Right?"

"That's where it's still fuzzy," Steven admitted. "Things might happen for a reason, *but why is the world like it is*?"

"That's a question that's been bothering you all your life." Vic spoke as if he could see Steven's thoughts and read his memories.

"And that's why Cham brought me to the spider. Cham was just throwing every one of my doubts back in my face, but Cham was really just a part of me. That means I'm holding to my doubts. I have to accept that. The problem is that I don't know what it means. While I understand why I came across Laura and had to face her suffering, why did I end up focusing so much on a spider?"

"Do you really think it was just the spider? Or was the spider just representing the last big unknown to you? As I said, you might need to look at the bigger picture here."

"I'm trying. I know there's something more here for me. I can almost see it, but it just won't come clear. What is it that I'm missing?"

"I don't think you're missing anything. I think you're just afraid to face the last question you have. You're worried it might feed your doubts as opposed to release them. You have to let go of that fear."

"I didn't think I had fears anymore." Steven knew this to be almost completely true. His soul touched many emotions, but fear was the one thing that seemed totally absent from him the moment he died. In fact, the only time fear was prevalent at all was when he was linked with the spider.

Vic, however, forced Steven to rethink that assumption. "Until you face this last reservation, fear is always going to be waiting to take you away from where you need to go. It's just a little less obvious now, but that doesn't make it any less present, or dangerous."

Was the fear hiding in the background? Was it holding Steven back from facing his last and perhaps most important issue with God?

"You think I'm afraid to face the truth?"

"On this one point, yes." Vic stated bluntly, but then offered more than a slice of solace. "Look, what you're afraid of is nothing to be ashamed of. You believe life isn't fair. And when you think that way, it's not you being selfish. You're not wondering why you weren't rich and famous or why you weren't more important. What bothers you is what was happening around you, not to you. And it didn't matter how insignificant the suffering or the creature. If anything, you were empathetic to the smallest of beings and that's a credit to you, but you still have to face up to the truth."

"Why is there suffering?" Steven asked aloud.

"That's really your question for God, isn't it?"

"Yes."

Vic smiled. "And now you have to face the answer, an answer that's already inside you. You've been with God. You've been in heaven and on earth. Open up your consciousness to what's in your soul. Don't be afraid."

Steven searched the new awareness that was now his. He opened his mind to the far reaching perception of his soul. He began to speak of what was now unfolding before him. The shadows of secret pain and the uncertainties of mystery dissolved away. "It's not just the suffering. It's the helplessness and the unhappiness. It's everywhere. You can ignore it, but you can't escape it. God is supposed to love us. He creates us and then sends us to earth where there is so much pain. Why were we put in a place that can be so cruel?"

Vic pressed Steven onward. "You're halfway there. You're facing what scares you the most, but you have to go the final step. You asked why God would send us to a place that is so cruel. The real question is why were any of us sent here in the first place? Not just you, or me, or Laura, or Raymond, but everyone and everything. Why did we all end up on earth? Why do we have to go through life here before we get to heaven?"

And with that question now spoken, Steven's understanding grew even more. "We chose to be here."

"That's right," Vic agreed, "but it goes even beyond that. Every single creature chooses to be here, including spiders. You know, some people believe that life starts right here on earth, but it doesn't. It starts in heaven, but we don't get to stay in heaven if we can't accept one simple thing."

"We have to accept God," Steven acknowledged. Even as a spirit standing on earth, he knew decisively God was with him, but he was not yet being totally honest with himself or God.

"That's really all there is to it," Vic replied, ready to guide Steven the last few steps. "It's no great mystery, no big puzzle you have to solve. Each and every one of us ended up on earth because we wanted to test the waters without Him. We wanted to see if we could make do on our own, or even worse, if we could do better."

"That's what I always thought," Steven admitted. "When I saw terrible things happen, I questioned God. I wanted to know how He could allow such things, but it went even beyond that.

I wanted to tell God to stop the pain, to make things better. I wanted to tell Him that He didn't know what He was doing. That's what Cham was talking about."

"That's what *you've* been thinking all your life. The only problem with that is that you placed the blame in the wrong place."

"That's what I'm starting to understand."

"It's easy to blame God for all the bad things here on earth, especially when we say He's responsible for everything. Truth is, God didn't make the rules for what happens here, we did. It had to be that way. It had to be that way because we were the one's that thought we could do better. He gave us exactly what we wanted. God might have created heaven and earth, but we set the way things work down here. And so things had to make sense in some logical way. There has to be an explanation for all things."

Steven repeated something Vic told him when they met in heaven. "We create our own purgatory and we choose to go to hell."

"Exactly," Vic confirmed. "The world had to represent *our* beliefs, not His. If you want to use the example of the spider, all I have to say is there are no insects in heaven. We brought misery and even evil into existence. He didn't. He wouldn't. When we decided we needed unhappiness so we could understand happiness, we created more pain than we could possibly imagine. God didn't create the suffering, we did. God might have created this world, but people made it into what it is. You already have the proof of that. Nature is cruel, and God would never have made anything like that."

"And so we come back to the spider."

"Not only the spider, but everything that happens here that we can't explain. We want to believe in God when we're here on earth, and then we run into one contradiction to His existence after another. Some people may want to call it a test, I just don't see it like that. It's more of a reminder of what can happen when we really reject God."

"And I almost rejected Him completely when I died."

"Don't be so hard on yourself. We may all choose to leave

God at one time or another, but we always have the chance to come back. That's the lesson from Laura. We face our demons, we learn our lessons, and we decide for ourselves what we want to believe. Even through all of that, we're not alone, even when we want to be. We get help when we really need it."

"Like I'm getting help from you now."

"It's a two-way street, Steven. I'm here just as much for myself as I am for you. I died before you were born. I never got the chance to be there for you. This was my chance to do something for you, and I'm grateful for the opportunity."

"And that's why you brought me to Raymond."

"God, through his messenger, made sure I brought you to Raymond. Like Laura said, He didn't give up on either of them. I just wanted to help you. The fact that I was able to guide you in a way that helped someone else just makes it all that much better."

And with that said, the last piece of the puzzle fell into place for Steven. He saw it all now, just as Laura did when Raymond was brought before her. Just as Raymond hopefully would at some point when he was ready to accept God.

"The truth is I never stopped blaming God. I thought I stopped before I died, but I didn't. I went on blaming Him even after I died. Deep down, I still blame Him now. Even after all I've seen and been through, I just can't help wondering why He doesn't make it all better for us. No matter how you cut it, that's still blaming Him. I really can't stop that, can I?"

"Not on your own. The question now is, are you going to face up to it all and ask for the help you need?"

"I really don't have to make a decision," Steven stated. "I already did when I opened the door. All I have to do now is understand what's right in front of me." He paused only for a moment as he looked down the river and then up at the few stars that became visible in twilight. "I accept this world for what it is, and I choose to leave it behind. Just one more place to go."

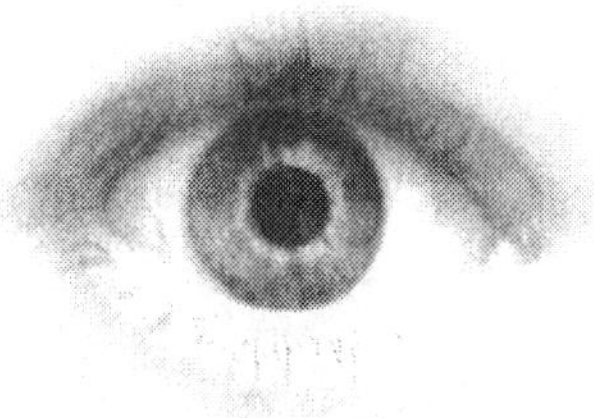

ACCEPTANCE

The river below and the stars above faded out of sight, and Vic and Steven left earth never to return. Upon this last transcendence into the spiritual existence of the afterlife, Steven willed himself not into heaven, but back into the empty room of the purgatory he created. It was, however, not totally empty. Cham waited stoically in the center of the room.

Vic patted Steven on the back. "I'll be here if you really need me, but I don't think you will."

Taking a bold step forward, Steven whispered back, "Thanks."

Cham did not smile upon Steven's return. If anything, a slight sneer bit at his lip. "So how's this all working out for you?"

"I know you're a part of me," Steven answered abruptly.

"Oh please, let's not start with that nonsense. You're not going to go on and on about how I'm just a manifestation of your doubts and all that other psycho babble, are you? I really don't want to hear it. It doesn't really matter what I am or what I represent. What matters is whether or not you can really face up to what I have to say? It was one thing to throw open the door of some mirage and say hello to God. It's another thing all together to walk up and shake the hand of the devil."

"You're right, it is."

"So where do you want to start with this?" Cham demanded, daring Steven to proceed.

"First, let me tell you about Laura."

"I don't need to hear about Laura. I'd rather hear about Raymond."

Not where he wanted to go, but Steven faced it anyway.

"Fine. Raymond found his mother."

"That's not all, is it?"

"No, it's not. He still can't accept his death, so he's still trapped back on earth."

"Taking on even more blame, no doubt. Torturing himself over an accident. That's basically what you've done for him, compounded his torture. He really wasn't totally sure if he killed his mother, but now he knows the truth."

"Yes, he does," Steven admitted without regret.

"And where does that bring him? Filled with more guilt than ever."

"That's his choice."

"And what's your choice? You're part of it, too. You helped free Laura, explained away all her misery. And where did it go? Right on Raymond's back. Misery doesn't go away, does it? It just gets moved from one person to another. So why don't we start there?"

"Looks like we already have."

"So what's the answer then, smart boy? You should have them all by now."

"Misery happens on earth, not in heaven, not with God. That's the answer."

"That's a pretty generic answer. I could have gotten that from any two-bit sidewalk preacher. Tell me something that's profound. Tell me something that will make all my doubts go away."

"I'm not supposed to make your doubts go away."

"My doubts are your doubts. Don't you remember that crap you said when you came in here? 'I know you're a part of me.' That's what you said. You can't have doubts when you face God."

And this truly was the last hurdle for Steven, whether or not he could face God without hiding his fears.

"But I can. I can have doubts about myself, even doubts about God. That's why I'm really here. I'm here to face it all. You were right. I blamed God and I still do. I guess that's as close to shaking hands with the devil that I can get."

"Nice to hear you admit it. And where does that put you now?"

"Accepting the truth."

"You're going in circles."

"Then let me try to get to the point. Just because I blame God, and admit it, doesn't mean I'm right. God doesn't deserve any blame."

"Now, you're not only going in circles, you're not even making sense. You admit you blame God, at the same time you tell me God isn't to blame."

"It's really not so confusing. I blame God because I'm angry and it makes sense. There are things that happen that I have no control over. There is suffering and I can't do a thing about it. God, however, is supposed to fix everything. That's what God is all about. In fact, the more you believe in Him, the easier it is to find fault. But the fault isn't with Him, the fault is with me, and that's what I accept."

"So what you're saying is that when something bad happens to someone it's no one's fault but their own. They deserve every tragedy that's heaped on them? Oh, I'm sure they're going to enjoy hearing that."

"No, I'm saying that we all asked for a chance to see what things are like without God. That's why we ended up on earth.

It's not a punishment. It's what we asked for. How can we blame God for that? He gave us exactly what we wanted."

"And that makes it okay? We asked for this world, so that lets God off the hook? Is that what you're saying? He gets to walk away, turn his back, and we have no right to complain."

"No, we can complain all we want, but even though I want to, even though I know I still do, I'm not justified in blaming God. And do you know what else? God won't let Himself off the hook. He doesn't turn his back on us and walk away. I learned that from Laura."

"And what did you learn from Raymond?"

"I learned that it's still up to us to decide if we want to be separated from God. That's really why I'm here. I'm going to reclaim my doubts. I'm going to accept that I've always had them. I'm not proud of them, but I won't try to refuse blame for them, either. They're mine, not yours, and not God's. I have to own up to them."

"So you're ready to walk up to God and blame Him for everything? I hope you're also ready for all those consequences we talked about."

Steven realized it was no use arguing with Cham. Cham would debate the issue forever. That's why he was there.

"What I'm ready to do now is take back from you everything I gave you. Even when I broke through my own personal barrier, I didn't go all the way through. I left you here. I tried to hide you from God, keep you in here and out of sight. Not very smart. All I managed to do was keep my own little purgatory open for business. I can't have that anymore. I'm going to accept my doubts, my fears, my faults, and return to God with them intact. Once I do that, I will erase you and this entire room from existence. I won't allow my purgatory to remain as a way out."

Cham's sneer became more pronounced. "What if I don't want to go away?"

"You really don't have a choice in the matter."

"Now you're getting rather bold."

"Actually, it's just the opposite. It's more like surrender. When I leave here to see God, I'm not marching in like some conquering hero. I'm not going to ask him questions about why the world is so cruel or demand explanations for why bad things happen. I'm going to ask for help. I'm going to tell Him I want to stop blaming Him, but I can't do it on my own. And that's what I've learned. I've learned I not only accept God, I need him."

"And just how are you going to leave here? Look around! There's no door in this room anymore."

"I already opened that door, so it's not important anymore. The door was about denying God. That's no longer a problem. The only problem left is you. You're the one keeping me from acknowledging I need God. I'm here to accept everything I am. When I do that, you'll be gone and so will this room."

Steven stepped closer to Cham.

Cham appeared uncertain, but said nothing.

"I'm taking them back," Steven declared. "I'm taking it all back. You can't keep it from me."

Cham did not fight against Steven's will. He couldn't. Cham's form changed into a dark shadow that cast upon the floor connected to Steven's feet. At first it grew, lengthening into a giant dark outline across the blank floor. Then it quivered and pulsated.

Feeling all the doubt and anger flow back into his soul, Steven did not resist. The shadow of Chamuel joined with him completely. It did not please Steven to welcome this sour darkness back into his essence, but he would not refuse it. He accepted it with shame and regret, but he acknowledged his flaws.

Vic stepped up to his grandson. "We can go now."

"Yes, we can," Steven agreed, and his purgatory melted away around him, this time forever.

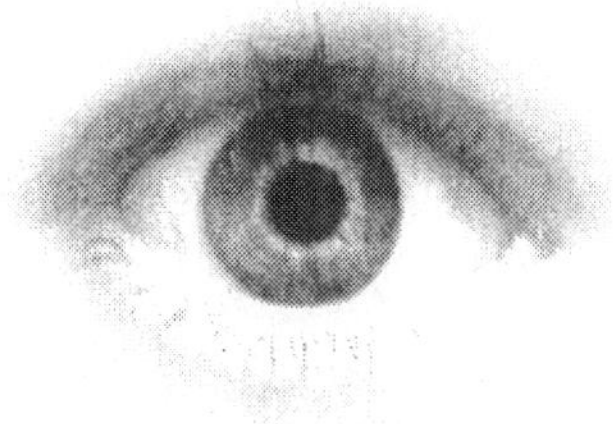

HEAVEN

In that first instant that his self-made purgatory dissolved, Steven finally and truly met with God. In the presence of his Creator, Steven did not try to hide his doubt, his anger, or his fear. He let it all show, not proud of these thoughts and emotions, but unwilling to deny them. As much as it shamed him, he revealed them to God, and without hesitation, he asked for help to remove them. He received that help without reservation, and he was welcomed into the folds of heaven.

This time, when Steven entered, he did so completely and the moment was profound. Triumphant music showered upon him and dazzling lights filled the skies. The doubt, anger, and fear that kept Steven from accepting his place in heaven dissolved. All of the barriers had been removed, and he felt a true sense of belonging.

As Steven immersed himself into an existence of enlightenment, God remained with him—a constant companion, a comforting presence, an everlasting embrace—and Steven came to know God as the essence of fulfillment.

God held to no anger and enabled no doubt. God brought

peace and erased fear. Torment, suffering, and pain could not exist in the presence of God. Truly, God encompassed more than the hopes of all man, for such hopes are bound by the imperfections of a mortal existence. God remained perfect, and thus, the hope within that perfection could not be flawed.

God was more than joy, more than bliss. In understanding the true essence of God, Steven realized that all the misery created on earth had nothing to do with God, but instead, everything to do with daring to refuse heaven. Accepting God allowed for a true freedom of spirit, a freedom to exist in paradise.

Heaven was not maintained by a balance of happiness against sadness, or even good against evil. In God, there was a purity of sheer benevolence. A soul in the presence of God received encouragement and reassurance beyond the bounds of the universe. Steven realized the very truth in what he learned. There could be no heaven without God, and within heaven, love from God was immeasurable. In return, all God asked for was acknowledgment and acceptance.

In this moment of pure enlightenment, Steven realized that it was the soul that was created in the image of God, and each spirit was fashioned not on earth, but in heaven itself. He had in every measure come home.

Allowing his imagination to fill the space that his spirit encompassed, Steven returned to the re-creation of his house that stood before the grand mountains of his creativity. He stood alongside Vic just off the front porch marveling at everything before him.

"How do you feel?" Vic asked his grandson.

"Better," Steven replied through emotions of joy that seemed to have no end. "No, it's more than that. It's like it's all been wiped clean. Everything that ever weighed me down before, it's gone. I understand it all now, and I want to leave it behind and never go back. It's the most free I've ever felt. It's like flying in heaven."

"That's where we are now, and you can fly if you want. Even

more, you can create any magical story you imagine. You can even create music again, but this time it won't be just you. God is here with you, as are the souls of so many friends you've never even met. Magic, music, and flying—no more blaming God, no more doubt about where you belong. Sound good?"

"Yes it does."

"Well like I said before, there's a great many people that want to say hello to you."

"And I want to meet them, but first I need to fly."

And Steven soared through the skies of his imagination—with God and without fear.

AUTHOR'S AFTERWORD

I'd like to take this opportunity to explain my perceptions of Steven's experience in the afterlife as a probable occurrence for a soul that carries doubts into the afterlife, but may not wish to acknowledge them. I would also like to stress that this book evolved into something much more than I originally intended.

The initial inspiration for the book came from a desire to describe the existence of an afterlife. I had hoped to focus on a description of heaven, and in doing so, I included interests that were of personal importance.

Music, fantastic adventures, the ability to fly; these are all objects of my heavenly desires, byproducts of my creativity and imagination. I never expected that these aspirations, as introduced through Steven's experience, would appeal to everyone, but I hoped they would be positive, diverse, and broad enough to capture the spirit of a heavenly existence. Utilizing these aspects was a way to define a spiritual existence beyond the boundaries of a mortal life. Still, even as I described Steven fulfilling his dreams, he remained unsatisfied with his predicament. It is here that the ultimate message of the book began to take shape.

When starting the book, I did not set out to focus on inner doubts or the idea of blaming God for the state of the world. Instead, I hoped to illustrate a transference into a spiritual plane. While my original intention was to focus on the aspects of heaven, the story itself led me to delve into deeper matters regarding an outlook of God. In many ways, Steven's experiences took on a life of their own as I wrote them. At first, I believed these aspects simply aided the flow of the narrative. As the story progressed, it expanded into a much deeper reflection of uncertainty and even denial toward God.

When I reviewed portions of what I had written, I realized certain points that I originally deemed somewhat trivial turned out to be unusually significant. The inclusion of the lost spirit trapped in the water was at first meant to be nothing more than a tool to describe an individual unable to accept death, a person caught between the two planes of existence. As the story developed, the woman in the river played a pivotal part in Steven's journey. The significance of this spirit had little to do with a description of an afterlife, but rather a revelation regarding inner doubt towards God.

There were other facets that were included with a specific purpose in mind, but these purposes changed along with the message of the book. The white room was a blank slate for Steven's imagination as well as an anchor for his soul. It allowed him to become comfortable with his surroundings as he grew to understand his new existence. The door was included as a simple construct to allow Steven to move beyond the limitations of his initial existence in a spiritual world.

As the message ultimately changed, the significance of these objects transformed as well. The white room became more of a prison and the door an obstacle. Steven had separated himself from God upon his death.

The actual existence of the door became extraordinarily critical. In retrospect, I could have depicted a room with absolutely no door at all, just stairways back to an earthly existence. The walls could have been otherwise completely solid. If that were the case, Steven would be entering the afterlife with potentially no willingness to accept the existence of God. There would have been no opportunity for Steven to ask Cham about the door, no moment of enlightenment when he realized he was, in fact, very close to God, separated merely by a closed door.

By including a door in this purgatory, Steven allowed for the opportunity to pass through the barrier. Unfortunately, when he constructed the room upon his arrival into the afterlife, Steven shut the door. He created the conflict within himself on whether he was truly ready to enter the presence of God. The door served as the decision. To open it meant not only accepting God, but entering a true heaven as opposed to the imaginary one he created in purgatory.

Once Steven moved past the white room, I had another opportunity to describe heaven, but instead I chose to return Steven to earth. As it turned out, he had still not fully accepted God. He had only been willing to break through a single barrier and was unwilling to face the truth of his own inner turmoil. Steven's grandfather led him back to the reservoir that in one way killed him and in another way helped save him. It was only after Steven returned to his self-made purgatory and accepted his doubts and his failings that he was ready to enter the presence of God.

With the story concluded, I found that my message went beyond the simple scope of depicting the transition into a spiritual existence or a description of heaven. Through Steven's journey, it is possible to connect his experience to any soul that eventually crosses to the spiritual world holding to uncertainties about God. We see pain in this world and we blame God. We create doubt in His existence, this doubt creates barriers, and these barriers must be overcome in order for us to find a true heaven. As Steven discovered during the time in his own purgatory, there is no heaven without God.

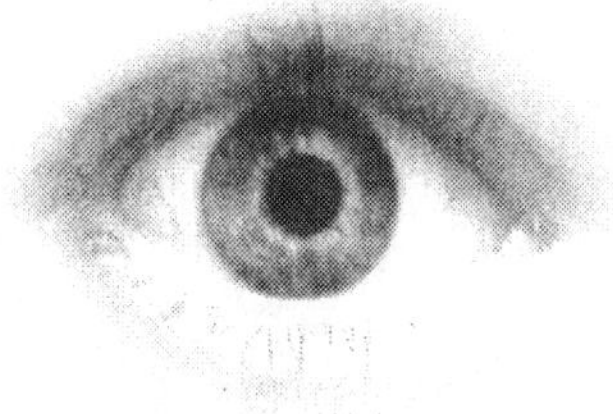

ABOUT THE AUTHOR

Jeff Ianniello earned his MBA from Farleigh Dickinson University and a Bachelor of Science degree in Finance from The College of New Jersey. While working as an accountant, he used his free time to write fantasy and science fiction. During the emergence of the Internet, he trained himself as a web developer. As he extended his creative abilities, he expanded the scope of his writing and ventured into spiritual concepts. He owes everything to his wife and soul mate, Joan, who has led him to understand the true meaning of destiny.

They currently live in New Jersey with their dog, Jilly.

Rainbow Ridge Books publishes spiritual and metaphysical titles, and is distributed by Square One Publishers in Garden City Park, New York.

To contact authors and editors, peruse our titles, and see submission guidelines, please visit our website at:

www.rainbowridgebooks.com.

For orders and catalogs, please call toll-free:
(877) 900-BOOK.